CALL THE MIDWIFE

THE OFFICIAL COOKBOOK

ANNIE GRAY

weldon**owen**

CONTENTS

FOOD IN BRITAIN 1956–1970

When *Call the Midwife* opens in 1956, the shadow of the Second World War still looms large. Children play in bomb sites, the housing situation is dire, and fourteen years of rationing and shortages have only just come to an end. Rationing casts a long shadow. The development of British cuisine had effectively stopped, and the food of the 1950s was very similar to that of the 1930s—at first. It didn't take long to catch up, however, and the late 1950s and the 1960s were characterized by both technological development and an enthusiasm for all the things that had been in short supply throughout the war.

The food of *Call the Midwife* reflects the context in which it is served, which is solidly working class. There were pockets of real poverty, and some families were desperately in need despite reforms to the welfare state. But in the main, rising living standards and high employment levels meant that working people ate reasonably well, even if many people maintained the habits of the war (and before), meaning that every scrap was used and economy was practiced as a matter of course.

One of the most notable foods in *Call the Midwife* is cake. In one of the very first scenes, Nurse Jenny Lee is stuffed full of cake by Sister Monica Joan. The cake chosen, a coconut layer cake, was one of screenwriter Heidi Thomas' family recipes, and it set the tone for many more confections to come. The foods in the show are drawn from memory, anecdote, and contemporary sources. The recipes in this book are also all based on specific sources from the time, reflecting current tastes rather than the modern evolution of some of the items involved. However, they've been carefully chosen and tweaked so they are as tasty to people today as they would have been to the residents of Poplar in the past.

In the 1950s, sugar consumption in Britain was the highest it has ever been, and the cakes and biscuits that you'll find in the first part of this book were everywhere. They were often ludicrously decorated with joie de vivre expressed through silver balls. However, they were generally smaller than those of today. Most cake recipes were based on a 6-inch (15-cm) cake pan, and the results would easily fit on a standard dinner plate.

Eggs and milk were staples, with the latter consumed not only fresh but also in tins of evaporated and condensed milk. Milk puddings were popular, custard was beloved by all, and milk was widely seen as vital for good health. In 1960, the average person got through five pints (six US pints) of milk a week and 227 eggs a year. Butter was the king of fats, though in poorer households, margarine was regarded as a good substitute. Lard remained important, as did meat drippings (both have a high smoke point, making them particularly good for frying). On the other hand, oil (olive or otherwise) was so rarely used that it barely even registered on the National Food Surveys at the start of the period.

In contrast to milk, meat consumption was much lower than it is today. In 2021, yearly consumption per person in Britain stood at 185 pounds (84 kg). In 1960, the average Briton ate 121 pounds (55 kg) per year. Beef was dominant, due partly to the historic focus on beef and Britishness. Fred's favorite dinner is steak. Mutton was also still enjoyed. Fish was surprisingly seldom eaten at home, but it reigned supreme as takeout, for fish-and-chips were as embedded in the British psyche as tea. During the war, they'd been seen as so important to morale that they'd never been rationed.

This book reflects home cooking and therefore doesn't include recipes for dishes like fish-and-chips. For the same reason, the Scotch eggs, pork pies, and jellied whelks that we see in the show aren't included, as they would all have been bought. The same applies to commercially available biscuits and cakes, such as the Battenberg cakes that fail to sell for the Buckles in

season 11. Both takeout and eating out boomed in the 1950s. We frequently see the fish-and-chip van, plus cafés and pie shops and the occasional higher-end restaurant.

One of the reasons for the proliferation of ready-made options was that cooking technology was also changing fast. At the start of the series in 1956, many of the homes still have large cast-iron ranges: hard to operate, expensive on fuel, and punishing in the summer. By season 11 (1967), most homes have gas or electric ovens with grills (US broilers). More homes also had fridges, and some even had freezers. Expenditure on frozen food quadrupled in the 1960s, though the majority of sales were to catering outlets.

Food shopping took a lot of time. In 1961, there were only eight thousand self-service grocers and only nine hundred supermarkets in the United Kingdom, rising fast to twenty-four thousand self-service stores and thirty-two hundred supermarkets by 1969. But these sources still accounted for only 60 percent of the total grocery trade. With limited storage in homes, and no means to keep things chilled, most people shopped every day on foot (car ownership was also low), buying just what was needed. Local shops—butchers, bakers, grocers, sweets shops, greengrocers—and market stalls were vital, as was the milkman. The recipes in this book reflect these shopping patterns. You can get the ingredients easily in a small grocer (today, admittedly, most likely to be a small branch of a supermarket rather than an independent outlet), and few things other than milk, cream, and meat require refrigeration.

Food presentation was different as well. You don't have to present the food you cook from this book in a period style, but it is quite good fun. Embrace the brown and the beige in food, but temper it with mass-produced plates using color and pattern. When it comes to cakes and sweets, forget subtlety, but also forget any ideas of what anything "should" look like. Learn to love sprinkles and lurid dyed fruits, marbled icing and crystallized flowers. The war is over, and according to Prime Minister Harold Macmillan, Britain has "never had it so good." Food may be kitsch, but it has in it innate joy that cannot be denied. So cook it, eat it, and revel in it.

RECIPE NOTES

The original recipes from which these dishes are taken were generally measured in ounces, both fluid and dry. Here, they've been redone to include two units of measure: US customary and metric. If you don't already have a digital scale, I strongly advise the purchase of one, especially for the baking recipes, where I find the metric measures yield the best results.

Temperatures are given in Fahrenheit and Celsius and assume a conventional oven. For convection (fan-assisted) ovens, lower the temperature by 10° to 25°F (5° to 15°C). Cakes and pastries always turn out best when baked with conventional heat.

Virtually every original 1950s and 1960s source for everyday food uses margarine instead of butter. However, there are some things, like polio and women dying in backstreet abortions, that should stay firmly in the past. I've replaced the margarine with butter in every case. It's nicer as well as better for you, and it is more predictable in cooking. I have used only salted butter unless specified otherwise. You can swap it for unsalted, adjusting the seasoning to taste. Remember that salt helps bring out flavors, and even cakes sometimes need a pinch to help them along the way.

All the eggs are US large (UK medium) unless otherwise noted, and all the milk is whole. If a recipe calls for simply "flour," use all-purpose (UK plain white). Some recipes specify whole-wheat (UK wholemeal) flour and bread (UK strong white bread) flour. When a recipe says "sugar," granulated white sugar is fine. Some cakes and other sweets and the occasional savory, however, need superfine (UK caster) sugar. Confectioners' (UK icing) sugar is often used for frostings, meringues, and finishing various cakes and other sweets. Occasionally brown sugar (if neither light nor dark is specified, either will work fine) and Demerara sugar are used as well. Salt is generic kosher salt (flaked salt in the UK) and pepper is black unless otherwise indicated.

I assume that anyone with specific dietary needs will be used to altering recipes to suit and will be able to do so here. The recipes, however, have been tested as written, so if you swap in cabbage for chicken or tomato sauce for cream and the recipe isn't great, please feel free not to write and tell me. Many of the recipes are vegetarian (it would be unfair to Nurse Crane otherwise) and can be made vegan with relative ease. The era was one that really embraced convenience, mainly in the form of tinned foods, so if you find it hard to chop or stand at the counter for long periods of time, don't hesitate to use frozen or tinned substitutes, ready-chopped vegetables, ready-made cake icing, and dehydrated shortcuts, such as bouillon powder, gravy granules, and custard powder.

Cooks used a lot of food coloring in the 1960s. I tend to use coloring in powder form, as it does not affect the liquid balance of the recipe (this is particularly important in icing, especially for piping). Gel coloring will also work in most cases, but the liquid stuff is best avoided.

For extracts (UK essences) and other flavorings, try to source all-natural products. This advice flies in the face of actual 1960s practice, but they do taste better. You may need to adjust the quantities needed depending on the strength of your flavoring.

Embrace the silver balls! Due to safety restrictions, hundreds and thousands and other such fripperies in the United Kingdom today are slightly more muted in color than they would have been in the 1960s (but on the plus side, less likely to cause hyperactivity). It was a bright and joyous time: More is more, and all of those little plastic toys and tooth-endangering toppings can (and indeed should) be used with carefree abandon.

PANTRY STAPLES

Suet: The hard fat from around the kidneys of cows and sheep, suet has long been an important ingredient of the UK kitchen. The leading brand in Britain is Atora, which comes in shredded form and is also available in some markets and online in the United States. Atora also markets a vegetarian suet. There are no good alternatives to suet.

Golden syrup and black treacle: A form of treacle, golden syrup is a thick, smooth, amber-color syrup made from cane sugar. The best-known brand is Lyle's (Tate & Lyle). There is no good substitute for golden syrup. Some recipes specify black treacle, which is molasses and is much darker and has a stronger flavor than golden syrup. In the United States, blackstrap molasses most closely approximates its flavor. Lyle's brand golden syrup and black treacle are available in well-stocked markets and online in the United States.

Baking powder: A mixture of bicarbonate of soda and cream of tartar (generally in a two-to-one ratio, with an optional extra one part cornstarch), baking powder is a leavener commonly used in cakes and biscuits. Do not confuse it with baking soda (UK bicarbonate of soda), which is also used in recipes in this book.

Mixed spice: A ready-made blend typically sold in jars and cellophane packets, mixed spice (the term goes back to the late Georgian period, so it has a well-established history) is a mixture of powdered sweet spices used in many traditional British baked goods. It generally contains allspice, cinnamon, nutmeg, mace, cloves, coriander, and ginger and is similar to the US pumpkin pie spice, which can be substituted. If you have neither on hand, you can mix up your own version, using cinnamon, allspice, nutmeg, coriander, and any other sweet spices in your pantry, blending them to suit your taste.

Puff pastry and shortcrust: When buying ready-made puff pastry, please make sure it is an all-butter brand. The artificial fat-based versions taste terrible. For shortcrust pastry, I've given instructions for making it, as it is so easy to do at home. But if you do choose to buy it, again, an all-butter brand is vital.

Bread: In recipes calling for bread, the best choice is properly yeasted bread—that is, from a bakery that uses yeast, salt, flour, water, and nothing else in its dough. The Chorleywood process, named for a village in southwest Britain, was invented in 1961, and slightly squidgy supermarket white sliced was therefore around by the later part of the series. However, while it just borders on okay in late-1960s sandwiches, it is pretty terrible for cooking with, including for making bread crumbs, as it has a very high water content and not a lot of flavor. If you like the flavor, you could use sourdough, but it makes a bit of an odd bread pudding, and it is highly inauthentic for the era.

EQUIPMENT

None of these recipes absolutely requires special equipment, and you will find that if you are not in the United Kingdom, fairy cake pans and a few other bits may elude you. Recipes are there for playing with, however, so adjust as you see fit.

I've used pudding molds (UK basins) in three different sizes: 2½ cups (600 ml), 4 cups (950 ml), and 5 cups (1.2 l). But any bowl that will hold an equal amount will do. If it is for steaming or baking, make sure it is heatproof.

Ideally, you will have a fairy cake pan for making the fairy or butterfly cakes on page 59. The cups in a fairy cake pan are quite small, usually ¾ inch (2 cm) deep and only 2¾ inches (7 cm) across. You will need paper liners (cases) to line them. Tips on substituting a US muffin pan are included with the recipe.

LARGE CAKES

SISTER MONICA JOAN

We anticipate a newcomer. And there is neither cake nor sweetmeats with which to welcome her.

SEASON 4: EPISODE 1

COCONUT LAYER CAKE

The very first cake we see in the very first episode of Call the Midwife *is a splendid coconut layer cake. Sister Monica Joan plies the newly arrived Jenny Lee with enough cake to make her sick, as they finish the entire thing, and it is only later that Jenny realizes it was intended for the whole staff. This one is based on one made by screenwriter Heidi Thomas' grandmother, who made two versions of coconut cake: one a single-layer cake topped with strips of candied citrus peel, and the other a three-layer cake, reserved for special occasions, with buttercream and a coating of coconut. For that opening episode, the team decided to use the latter, more impressive version. It's characteristically moist and dense, with a sugar hit from the topping. Coating cakes in shredded dried coconut, which was very popular in the era, screams 1950s. However, you could also make the more muted version, using the cracks on the top of the cake to hold strips of candied citrus peel in place.*

SERVES 10–12

To make the cake, preheat the oven to 350°F (180°C). Butter the bottom and sides of an 8-inch (20-cm) round cake pan that is 3 inches (8 cm) deep. Sift together the flour and baking soda into a bowl. In a large bowl, using an electric mixer, beat together the butter and superfine sugar on medium speed until the mixture is light in color and fluffy. On low speed, add the flour mixture in three batches alternately with the eggs in two batches, beginning and ending with the flour and mixing well after each addition. Add the coconut and stir to mix well, then stir in the milk to slacken the mixture, again mixing well. Transfer the batter to the prepared pan.

Bake the cake for 1¼ hours, covering the top with aluminum foil if it begins to brown too much. The cake is done when the top is domed and slightly cracked and a skewer inserted into the center comes out clean. Let cool in the pan on a wire rack for 10 minutes, then turn the cake out onto the rack, turn the cake upright, and let cool completely.

When you are ready to assemble the cake, you can either dust the top of the single layer with the confectioners' sugar and lay the strips of candied peel in the cracks, or you can split the cake into three layers and fill and ice it with buttercream.

To make the buttercream, sift the confectioners' sugar into a bowl. Add the butter and vanilla and, using the electric mixer, beat on medium speed until the mixture is smooth and spreadable (it will be quite thick).

FOR THE CAKE

1 cup (225 g) butter, at room temperature, plus more for the pan

3 cups (370 g) flour

1½ teaspoons baking soda

1 cup plus 2 tablespoons (225 g) superfine sugar

3 eggs, lightly beaten with a fork

1½ cups (115 g) unsweetened shredded dried coconut

⅔ cup (160 ml) milk

FOR THE BUTTERCREAM (OPTIONAL)

3¼ cups (370 g) confectioners' sugar

¾ cup (170 g) butter, at room temperature

2 teaspoons pure vanilla extract

TO FINISH

1½ teaspoons confectioners' sugar and 6–9 strips candied lemon or orange peel, if making single-layer cake

1 cup (80 g) unsweetened shredded dried coconut, if making three-layer cake

Recipe continues on the following page

Continued from the previous page

Using a long, serrated knife, carefully cut the cake horizontally into three layers. Place the bottom layer on a cake plate and, using a palette knife or an offset spatula, spread it with a thin layer of the buttercream. Top with the middle layer and spread it with a thin layer of the buttercream. Then set the top layer in place, and cover the top and sides of the cake with the remaining buttercream. To finish, coat the top and sides of the cake with the coconut, gently pressing it onto the sides so it adheres.

SISTER EVANGELINA
There is nothing in this pot but crumbs!

CYNTHIA
But Mrs. B. made one this morning! I saw her when I came in from my delivery in Mitre Street!

SISTER EVANGELINA
I know she did! It was coconut, which is a very insinuating ingredient, liable to smear itself all over the consumer's face!

SEASON 1:
EPISODE 1

COFFEE AND WALNUT CAKE

Layer cakes are almost as frequent at Nonnatus House as ladders (runs) in Nurse Corrigan's stockings. Both coffee-flavored cakes and walnut cakes were stalwarts in the 1950s and 1960s, appearing without fail in cookery books and pamphlets. Many were the standard recipe of a basic Victoria sponge flavored with coffee extract or iced with a coffee glaze, with some token walnuts for decoration. This sponge is based on one published in 1958 by Georgina Landemare, cook to Winston and Clementine Churchill from 1940 to 1956. The denizens of Nonnatus House watch Winston Churchill's funeral procession at the start of season 9 (it took place in January 1965). Landemare trained in the Edwardian era, and the recipe reflects her time as a society chef in the 1930s. The topping, which relies on Camp Coffee (see 1960s Spin) for flavor, is pure 1960s.

SERVES 8–10

To make the cake, preheat the oven to 325°F (165°C). Butter the bottom and sides of a 7-inch (18-cm) round cake pan, then dust with a mixture of equal parts flour and superfine sugar, tapping out the excess. Line the bottom of the pan with parchment paper.

Sift together the flour and baking powder into a bowl. In a large bowl, using an electric mixer, beat together the butter and superfine sugar on medium speed until the mixture is light in color and fluffy. Add the eggs, one at a time, along with a tablespoon of the flour mixture with each egg to prevent the mixture from curdling, beating well after each addition. Once the eggs are thoroughly incorporated, using a rubber spatula, fold in the remaining flour mixture along with the walnuts and the Camp Coffee. Transfer the batter to the prepared pan.

Bake the cake until a skewer inserted into the center comes out clean, 45–60 minutes. Let cool in the pan on a wire rack for 5–10 minutes, then turn the cake out onto the rack, peel off the parchment, turn the cake upright, and let cool completely.

While the cake is baking, make the custard buttercream so it can cool completely before using. In a saucepan, combine the granulated sugar and milk over medium heat and bring to just below boiling point, stirring occasionally to dissolve the sugar. Meanwhile, in a bowl, whisk the egg yolks until blended. Remove the hot milk mixture from the heat and slowly pour it into the yolks while whisking constantly. Return the milk–egg yolk mixture to the pan over low heat and heat gently, whisking occasionally, until the mixture thickly coats the back of a spoon, about 5 minutes. Do not allow it to boil. Remove from the heat. Lightly butter a round of parchment paper and gently press it, buttered side down, onto the surface of the mixture to stop a skin from forming. Let cool for a few minutes, then refrigerate until chilled and thickened, about 1 hour.

FOR THE CAKE

¾ cup plus 1 tablespoon (185 g) butter, plus more for the pan

1½ cups (185 g) flour, plus more for the pan

¾ cup plus 2½ tablespoons (185 g) superfine sugar, plus more for the pan

1 teaspoon baking powder

3 eggs

1 cup (115 g) chopped walnuts

2 tablespoons Camp Coffee (see 1960s Spin)

FOR THE CUSTARD BUTTERCREAM

¼ cup (50 g) granulated sugar

½ cup plus 1½ tablespoons (140 ml) milk

2 egg yolks

¾ cup (170 g) unsalted butter, at room temperature, plus more for the parchment paper

1½ tablespoons Camp Coffee

FOR THE GLAZE AND TO FINISH

½–1 teaspoon Camp Coffee

½ cup (55 g) confectioners' sugar

16–20 walnut halves

When the custard has chilled and thickened, beat in the butter, a little at a time, ensuring it is well mixed after each addition before adding more. Toward the end, add the Camp Coffee, beating until the buttercream is smooth and thick.

To make the glaze, put ½ teaspoon of the Camp Coffee into a bowl, then sift the confectioners' sugar into the bowl and mix it with the coffee, adding more coffee if needed to achieve a loose piping consistency.

To assemble the cake, using a long, serrated knife, carefully cut the cake horizontally into two layers. Place the bottom layer on a cake plate. Using a palette knife or an offset spatula, spread the layer with about one-third of the buttercream. Place the second layer on top of the buttercream and then spread the remaining buttercream on top. Spoon the glaze into a piping bag fitted with a small plain tip and pipe the glaze on top of the cake in a checkerboard pattern with 32–40 squares. If it drips off the sides slightly, that's fine. Finally, place the walnut halves on top, putting one in every other square.

 1960s SPIN *Camp Coffee is a proprietary brand. A concentrated syrup, it is a mixture of chicory and coffee extracts and sugar syrup and, according to its original makers, R. Paterson & Sons Litd. of Glasgow, was invented in the late nineteenth century to supply the Gordon Highlanders with a coffee drink for field campaigns in India. It was also sold as instant coffee to a wider audience. By the 1960s, however, after the invention of freeze-dried instant coffee in the late 1930s, its main use was as a flavoring for cakes—at which it excels. There were other brands around in the 1960s, including Bev, advertised as "the best coffee drink in a bottle," but most of them have since disappeared from UK shelves. If you can't get hold of Camp Coffee, use instant coffee or chicory coffee mixed with sugar syrup (use 1 teaspoon instant coffee, 2 teaspoons superfine sugar, and 2 tablespoons water).*

SISTER MONICA JOAN
Today's layer cake assumes the form of coffee and walnut sponge. Since the maker's hand moved freely with the flavourings, I consumed my portion earlier, lest it render me wakeful tonight.
SEASON 6: EPISODE 4

SHERRY CAKE

Sherry is everywhere in Call the Midwife. *It was a hugely popular drink, both in pubs and in the home, and brands such as Tio Pepe were household names. Admittedly, toward the end of the era, it had started to gain a reputation as the choice drink for a maiden aunt—hence Miss Higgins' bonding with Nurse Crane over the stereotypical glass of sherry and unwanted bath bombs as the inevitable fate for older spinsters in the season 10 Christmas special. You don't have to use sherry for this cake. Any fortified wine will work, including ginger wine, port, or Madeira. Likewise, feel free to vary the color of the macaroons.*

SERVES 6–8

Start by making the macaroons. Preheat the oven to 350°F (180°C). Line two sheet pans with parchment paper and lightly butter the paper, or line each pan with a silicone baking mat.

In a bowl, whisk the egg whites until foamy. Then gradually add the sugar while continuing to whisk until stiff peaks form, adding the almond extract and food coloring along with the last of the sugar. (The egg whites can also be beaten with an electric mixer, starting on medium speed and increasing the speed to medium-high once the whites have thickened.) The pink shade should be on the lurid side to truly channel the era. Gently fold in the almonds just until evenly incorporated.

Scoop about one-third of the egg white mixture onto the center of a prepared sheet pan. Using the back of a spoon and a dampened rubber spatula, spread the mixture into a circle about 7 inches (18 cm) in diameter and about 1/4 inch (6 mm) thick. Use the rest of the egg white mixture to make smaller macaroons on the second prepared sheet pan. Each macaroon should be 1¾ inches (4 cm) or smaller in diameter and about 1/4 inch (6 mm) thick. (You can also use a piping bag to shape the macaroons on the sheet pans, using a large plain tip for the large macaroon and a small tip for the small macaroons.)

Bake the small macaroons for 15–20 minutes and the large macaroon for 25–30 minutes. They are ready when they are hard at the edges but still slightly soft in the center. Let them cool completely on the pans on wire racks. Leave the oven set at 350°F (180°C).

To make the cake, butter the bottom and sides of a 7-inch (18-cm) round cake pan, then dust with a mixture of equal parts flour and sugar, tapping out the excess. In a bowl, whisk together the eggs and sugar until a light, pale froth forms. Sift the flour and salt directly into the bowl, then fold in the ground almonds gently with a rubber spatula until incorporated. Pour the batter into the prepared pan.

FOR THE MACAROONS

Butter, at room temperature, for the pans (optional)

2 egg whites

2/3 cup plus 1 tablespoon (140 g) superfine sugar

Few drops of pure almond extract

Pink food coloring, preferably in powder form

FOR THE CAKE

Butter, at room temperature, for the pan

2/3 cup (85 g) flour, plus more for the pan

1/3 cup plus 1½ tablespoons (85 g) superfine sugar, plus more for the pan

2 eggs

Pinch of fine sea salt

1 cup plus 1½ tablespoons (110 g) ground almonds

FOR THE BUTTERCREAM

1/4 lb (110 g) cream cheese, at room temperature

2 tablespoons butter, at room temperature

3/4 cup (150 g) superfine sugar

1/4 cup (60 ml) sherry

Silver balls, for decorating

Recipe continues on the following page

Continued from the previous page

Bake the cake until the top is light brown and a skewer inserted into the center comes out clean, 35–40 minutes. Let cool in the pan on a wire rack for 15 minutes, then turn the cake out onto the rack, turn the cake upright, and let cool completely.

To make the buttercream, in a bowl, whisk together the cream cheese, butter, and sugar until a spreadable paste forms. Add the sherry very gradually, whisking well after each addition to stop the mixture from curdling. (If it does curdle, very briefly heat the buttercream in a microwave or, better still, place the bowl over a pan of boiling water to warm it a little.)

To assemble the cake, place the large macaroon on a serving plate. Using a palette knife or an offset spatula, spread a thin coating of the buttercream over the macaroon and then set the cake on top. (The buttercream helps keep the cake stuck in place.) Cover the top and sides of the cake with the remaining buttercream. To finish, decorate the top of the frosted cake with the small macaroons along with the inevitable silver balls.

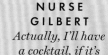

NURSE GILBERT
Actually, I'll have a cocktail, if it's all the same to you. Vicars' wives drink quite a lot of sherry, and I think it's time I got myself in training.

SEASON 6:
EPISODE 1

CHOCOLATE BUTTON CAKE

One of the more endearing characteristics of the 1950s and 1960s was the sheer level of enthusiasm for over-the-top, throw-everything-at-them cakes. It came tempered with an awareness that many home cooks were pressed for time and lacked culinary skills, never having been properly taught due to the years of making do during the war. And it also came with a readiness to rely on proprietary ingredients that were available in every corner shop, even if they weren't already pantry staples. This cake is a very good example, reliant as it is on evaporated milk—or "evap" as it was usually known. It's a widely referenced product in the show and is the subject of debate in season 4 as Sister Evangelina learns that breast isn't always best.

SERVES 10

To make the cake, preheat the oven to 350°F (180°C). Butter the bottom and sides of two 8-inch (20-cm) round cake pans, then dust with flour, tapping out the excess.

Sift together the flour, superfine sugar, cocoa powder, and baking powder into the bowl of a stand mixer. Stir in the salt. Fit the mixer with the paddle attachment, then, on low speed, add the butter about 1 tablespoon at a time, beating after each addition for several seconds, until all the butter is incorporated. The mixture should look evenly moistened and will be clumpy. In a small bowl, whisk the eggs just until blended, then whisk in the evaporated milk, water, and vanilla. On low speed, gradually add the egg mixture to the flour-butter mixture and beat just until incorporated. Stop the mixer and scrape down the sides of the bowl. On medium speed, continue to beat the batter, stopping to scrape down the bowl as needed, until the batter lightens in color and is fluffy, 5–8 minutes. Divide the batter evenly between the prepared pans.

Bake the cake layers until a skewer inserted into the center comes out clean, 25–30 minutes. Let cool in the pans on wire racks for 10 minutes, then turn the layers out onto the racks, turn them upright, and let cool completely.

To make the filling, in a bowl, beat together the butter and confectioners' sugar until smooth and spreadable. Put the chocolate into a small heatproof bowl, place over (not touching) simmering water in a small saucepan, and heat, stirring occasionally, until melted and smooth (or melt in a microwave). Beat the melted chocolate into the butter-sugar mixture, mixing well, then let cool to room temperature.

Place a cooled cake layer on a serving plate. Using a palette knife or an offset spatula, spread the top evenly with the filling. Top with the second cake layer. Set aside while you make the icing.

FOR THE CAKE

1 cup (225 g) unsalted butter, at room temperature, plus more for the pans

1½ cups (190 g) flour, plus more for the pans

1 cup plus 2 tablespoons (225 g) superfine sugar

2 tablespoons unsweetened cocoa powder

1 teaspoon baking powder

½ teaspoon salt

2 eggs

5 tablespoons (75 ml) evaporated milk

5 tablespoons (75 ml) water

1 teaspoon pure vanilla extract

FOR THE FILLING

3 tablespoons unsalted butter, at room temperature

½ cup (55 g) confectioners' sugar

1 oz (30 g) milk chocolate

Recipe continues on the following page

Continued from the previous page

To make the fudge icing, first melt the chocolate over simmering water as you did for the filling and set aside. In a small, heavy saucepan, melt the butter over medium heat, then add the evaporated milk and sugar and stir until the sugar has dissolved. Attach a candy thermometer to the side of the pan, raise the heat to medium-high, and heat, stirring occasionally, until the thermometer registers 235°–240°F (113°–116°C), known as the soft-ball stage. Add the melted chocolate and the vanilla, and stir vigorously until the mixture comes together and thickens.

Working quickly, pour the icing over the cake, encouraging it to drip down the sides. You can help it along with a heat-resistant rubber spatula, gently covering the sides.

Let cool for 15 minutes, until the icing is almost set and is no more than lukewarm (otherwise it will melt the chocolate buttons). Finally, decorate the top and the sides with the chocolate buttons and the chocolate sprinkles, if using. Let cool completely and set before serving.

 1960s SPIN *You can make this cake without the chocolate buttons and just use the icing to create different effects. One recipe for fudge icing suggests you pour it on top slowly and artistically, "leaving the surface in attractive swirls."*

FOR THE FUDGE ICING

2 oz (60 g) dark chocolate

4 tablespoons (60 g) butter

¾ cup (180 ml) evaporated milk

½ cup (55 g) granulated sugar

Few drops of pure vanilla extract

TO DECORATE

Chocolate buttons, in any color

Chocolate sprinkles or silver balls (optional)

> **MOTHER 1**
> *Americans are foreign. They do it all different!*
>
> **MOTHER 2**
> *You probably can't even get Carnation evaporated milk over there, I was reared on the stuff. My baby's getting the same.*
>
> SEASON 4:
> EPISODE 1

ANGEL CAKE

In Britain, angel cake is a confusing thing. There are two distinctly different cakes known by the name. One is a very fluffy, egg white–based, and fatless sponge that was introduced in the 1880s and usually appears in recipe books prefaced with the stern warning that this is an American cake (and not to be mistaken for the denser confections more familiar to Brits). The other is a multicolor, multiflavor layer cake that seems to have been developed in the 1950s mainly as a commercial cake, exploding into popular consciousness over the next few decades and being voted cake of the year in 1986. By then it was usually made from a standard sponge in oblong or square pans ideal for cutting into equal pieces to sell. The layers were invariably yellow, pink, and white. The American version— more properly called angel food cake—predated the colored one by at least sixty years, however, and the first mentions of the colored ones suggest that they were made of angel food cake, just with a fun twist. They almost certainly became the standard sponge because the sales appeal lay in the colors and flavors, not the cake itself, and standard sponges are much easier to make. In the spirit of the original angel cakes, this one is made with angel food cake—a double angel cake, if you like.

SERVES 8–10

It is easiest to make this cake in three separate lots so you do not inadvertently overmix the batter or fail to divide it evenly. See the Recipe Note for directions.

Preheat the oven to 350°F (180°C).

Sift together the flour, confectioners' sugar, and salt into a bowl, then sift again. In a large bowl, using an electric mixer, beat the egg whites on medium speed until they start to foam. Add one-third of the superfine sugar and beat until the whites are opaque. Add another third of the sugar and the cream of tartar, and continue beating. When the whites start to increase in volume and become firm, add the remaining sugar and the vanilla, increase the speed to high, and beat just until the whites form very soft peaks.

Divide the egg white mixture into thirds, putting each third into its own bowl, then beat in the relevant extract and powdered coloring. The vanilla cake should be left plain, the raspberry one should be colored pink, and the lemon one should be yellow. Add the coloring gradually, stopping when the color is vibrant. Do not overbeat. Divide the flour mixture into thirds. You will use one-third for each bowl of egg white mixture.

Sift one-third of a flour portion over the vanilla cake bowl and fold in with a rubber spatula. Sift and fold in the remaining flour mixture in two more additions, mixing just until evenly incorporated. Repeat with the remaining two flour portions, adding them to the raspberry and lemon cake bowls the same way. Pour each bowl of batter into an ungreased 9-inch (23-cm) round cake pan (a springform pan is fine) and smooth the top with the spatula.

FOR THE CAKE

1 cup (125 g) flour

1 cup (125 g) confectioners' sugar

¼ teaspoon salt

12 extra-large egg whites

¾ cup plus 1½ tablespoons (170 g) superfine sugar

1½ teaspoons cream of tartar

½ teaspoon pure vanilla extract

½ teaspoon pure raspberry extract

½ teaspoon pure lemon extract

Pink and yellow food coloring, in powdered form

FOR THE CUSTARD BUTTERCREAM

¼ cup (50 g) granulated sugar

½ cup plus 1½ teaspoons (140 ml) milk

1 tablespoon cornstarch

2 extra-large egg yolks

¾ cup (170 g) unsalted butter, at room temperature, plus more for the parchment paper

Bake the cake layers until the tops are lightly browned and feel springy when touched and a skewer inserted into the center comes out clean, 40–45 minutes. Invert the cakes in their pans onto racks or a countertop and let cool completely. Once cool, gently ease each cake layer out of its pan. You will probably need to loosen the bottom carefully with a knife.

While the cake layers are baking, make the custard buttercream so it can cool completely before using. In a saucepan, combine the granulated sugar and all but 2 tablespoons of the milk over medium heat and bring to just below the boiling point, stirring until the sugar dissolves. Meanwhile, in a small bowl, whisk together the reserved 2 tablespoons milk and the cornstarch until a paste forms. (You can skip this step if you are a confident custard maker and just heat all the milk with the sugar and omit the cornstarch.) In a medium bowl, whisk the egg yolks until blended. Remove the hot milk mixture from the heat and slowly pour it into the yolks while whisking constantly. Return the milk–egg yolk mixture to the pan and whisk in the cornstarch mixture. Return the pan to medium heat and heat gently, stirring constantly, until the mixture thickens, about 5 minutes. Do not allow it to boil. Remove from the heat. Lightly butter a round of parchment paper and gently press it, buttered side down, onto the surface of the mixture to stop a skin from forming. Let cool for a few minutes, then refrigerate until chilled and thickened, about 1 hour.

When the custard has chilled and thickened, beat in the butter, a little at a time, ensuring it is well mixed after each addition before adding more. The buttercream should be smooth and thick.

To assemble the cake, place the yellow cake layer on a serving plate. Using a palette knife or an offset spatula, spread the top evenly with half of the buttercream. Top with the pink cake layer and spread with the remaining buttercream. Set the white layer on top. There is no need to ice the top or sides. When serving, use a serrated knife to cut the cake to ensure it does not tear.

RECIPE NOTE To make the batter in three separate batches, use the following amounts for each cake: ½ cup (55 g) flour, ½ cup (55 g) confectioners' sugar, pinch of salt, 4 extra-large egg whites, ¼ cup (50 g) superfine sugar, ½ teaspoon cream of tartar, and the raspberry and lemon extracts as listed. Follow the same steps given for a single batch except for dividing the batter into thirds. If you have three cake pans, great! If you don't, let each cake cool completely before making the next. Remember to wash and dry the pan between uses.

You will end up with a lot of egg yolks, so embrace your inner custard fiend and have a go at the Banana Flowerpots (page 164) or the Rhubarb Crumble (page 168). Or just pour custard on bananas and settle down in front of the latest episode of *Call the Midwife*.

SISTER JULIENNE

We'll take care of the formalities later. I'm sure that first you'd like some tea and cake.

SEASON 1: EPISODE 1

CHOCOLATE CAKE WITH CHOCOLATE ICING

Every self-respecting cook needs at least one rich and satisfying chocolate cake in her or his repertoire. We never meet the elusive "Mrs. B," the cook responsible for at least some of the Nonnatus House catering, but given that she's clearly an established part of the wider Nonnatus family when the series starts in 1956, she probably learned much of her trade before the war. Old-school cookery writers of the 1950s had a tendency to lament the passing of the days of country house–trained cooks, who never had to worry over cost or scarcity of ingredients, and who could whip up a solid sponge without recourse to an instructional manual. This cake did the rounds of the comfortably well-off country house folk in the 1920s and 1930s—not the titled aristocrats so much as the rank just below them, families like that of Sister Monica Joan. Dorothy Allhusen included a recipe for just such a chocolate cake in her A Book Of Scents And Dishes, *attributing it to the late Lady Blanche Hozier (Clementine Churchill's mother), but it appeared, virtually without alteration, in a number of published and unpublished books of the time. It was originally served either undecorated or iced with a simple translucent water ice, but it's important to move with the times.*

SERVES 10

To make the cake, preheat the oven to 275°F (135°C). Butter the bottom and sides of an 8-inch (20-cm) springform pan, then line the bottom with parchment paper.

Put the chocolate into a heatproof bowl, place over (not touching) simmering water in a saucepan, and heat, stirring occasionally, until melted and smooth (or melt in a microwave). Let cool. Sift together the flour, sugar, and baking powder into a bowl. In a second bowl, beat the egg yolks until blended.

In a large bowl, beat the butter with a wooden spoon (or with an electric mixer on medium speed) until light in color and fluffy. Stir in the egg yolks until well mixed, then add the flour mixture and mix well. Stir in the almonds and then the chocolate, mixing well after each addition. Finally, in a medium bowl, using an electric mixer on medium-high speed or a whisk, beat the egg whites until stiff peaks form. Using a rubber spatula, gently stir about one-fourth of the egg whites into the chocolate mixture to lighten it, then gently fold in the remaining whites just until no white streaks remain. Transfer the batter to the prepared pan and give the pan a few taps on a countertop to settle the batter.

FOR THE CAKE

1 cup (225 g) butter, at room temperature, plus more for the pan

8 oz (225 g) high-quality dark chocolate, preferably 70–75 percent cacao, coarsely chopped

1 cup (125 g) flour

1 cup plus 2 tablespoons (225 g) superfine sugar

1 teaspoon baking powder

6 eggs, separated

1 cup plus 2 tablespoons (115 g) ground almonds

FOR THE DARK CHOCOLATE ICING

1½ cups (170 g) confectioners' sugar

3 oz (90 g) dark chocolate

½ teaspoon butter

1–2 tablespoons boiling water

Bake the cake until a skewer inserted into the center comes out clean, about 1½ hours. Let cool in the pan on a wire rack for 15–20 minutes, then open the clasp on the pan sides and let the cake cool completely. Lift off the pan sides and carefully invert the cake onto the rack. Lift off the bottom and peel off the parchment, then set the cake upright on a serving plate.

To ice the cake, first make the dark chocolate icing. Sift the confectioners' sugar into a large bowl. Put the chocolate into a heatproof bowl, place over (not touching) simmering water in a saucepan, and heat, stirring occasionally, until melted and smooth (or melt in a microwave). Add the chocolate, butter, and 1 tablespoon of the boiling water to the sugar and beat with a wooden spoon, adding more boiling water as needed to achieve a thick, smooth icing that coats the coats the back of the spoon and drips off very slowly when the spoon is lifted. Working quickly, as the icing sets almost immediately, pour the icing over the top of the cake. It should cover the top evenly and flow down the sides, coating them. If necessary, use a rubber spatula dipped in hot water to help smooth the icing on the sides.

To finish the cake, following the instructions for the dark chocolate icing, make the white chocolate icing. Spoon the icing into a piping bag fitted with a small plain tip and pipe neat parallel lines across the top of the cake. Let the icing set completely before serving.

FOR THE WHITE CHOCOLATE ICING

⅔ cup (85 g) confectioners' sugar

1¼ oz (35 g) white chocolate

½–1 tablespoon boiling water

CYNTHIA
Well, I'm hardly an expert when it comes to men, but I'm fairly sure that chocolate usually takes the edge off when things go wrong.

SEASON 3: EPISODE 3

STRAWBERRY MERINGUE CAKE

This cake combines two Call the Midwife *preferred desserts: fruit layer cakes and meringues. Meringues are one of Trixie's favorites, but she isn't the only one. We see Chummy making them to impress her mother when she introduces her to Peter in season 1, and both Nurse Mount and Sister Monica Joan are stopped in their tracks at various times by meringue-based desserts. Fred also woos Violet with them in season 4. Meanwhile, there's a raspberry layer cake to celebrate Delia's success talking a woman through labor in season 5, and a strawberry version during the tension of the Cuban missile crisis in season 6. You could, of course, just make a sponge cake with plain buttercream and add some fruit, but this 1964 recipe has a satisfyingly jubilant feel to it, just right for a celebration. The original suggests you can use tinned fruit, but fresh is much better. If, like Fred, you have strawberries on your allotment, great. Otherwise, any zingy fruit will work.*

SERVES 10

To make the cake, preheat the oven to 350°F (180°C). Line the bottom and sides of two 9-inch (23-cm) round cake pans with parchment paper and butter the parchment liberally.

Sift together the flour and baking powder into a bowl. In a second bowl, beat the egg yolks with a fork just until blended, then lightly beat in the milk and vanilla. In a large bowl, using an electric mixer, beat together the butter and superfine sugar on medium speed until the mixture is light in color and fluffy. On low speed, add the flour mixture in three batches alternately with the yolk mixture in two batches, beginning and ending with the flour mixture and mixing well after each addition. Divide the batter evenly between the prepared pans.

To make the meringue, wash and dry the electric mixer beaters well. Then, in a large bowl, using the electric mixer, beat together the egg whites and cream of tartar on medium speed until foamy. Increase the speed to medium-high and gradually add the superfine sugar, a little at a time, beating well after each addition, until soft peaks form. Then sift in the confectioners' sugar and continue to beat until stiff peaks form. Gently spoon the meringue on top of the batter in the cake pans, dividing it evenly and making the edges slightly higher than the middle. (Or you can use a piping bag fitted with a plain tip to pipe it onto the cake batter.) Sprinkle one meringue evenly with the almonds.

FOR THE CAKE

4 tablespoons (60 g) butter, at room temperature, plus more for the pan

1 cup (125 g) flour, sifted

1 teaspoon baking powder

4 egg yolks

½ teaspoon pure vanilla extract

5 tablespoons (75 ml) milk

½ cup plus 1 tablespoon (115 g) superfine sugar

FOR THE MERINGUE

4 egg whites

Pinch of cream of tartar

1 cup (200 g) superfine sugar

1 cup (115 g) confectioners' sugar

2 tablespoons sliced almonds or slivered blanched almonds

TO FINISH

¾ lb (340 g) fresh strawberries

2 teaspoons fresh lemon juice

1 cup (240 ml) heavy cream

Candied angelica and glacé cherries (optional)

Recipe continues on the following page

Continued from the previous page

Bake the cake layers until the meringue is hard and golden and the cake is cooked through, 40–45 minutes. To test the cake for doneness, stick a skewer through the meringue and into the cake. It should come out clean. Keep an eye on the layers toward the end of baking, as one may cook more quickly than the other. Don't worry if the meringue cracks. Let the layers cool in the pans on wire racks to room temperature, then turn them out on onto the racks, peel off the parchment, and turn upright.

To finish, stem and slice most of the strawberries, drop them into a bowl, and sprinkle and then toss them gently with the lemon juice. In a second bowl, whisk the cream by hand or with the electric mixer until stiff peaks form. Set the plain meringue layer on a serving plate and spread evenly with the cream. Layer the sliced strawberries on top of the cream. Top with the almond meringue. Stem and slice the remaining strawberries (keep a strawberry or two whole for decorating the center if you like) and use them to decorate the top. You can also add strips of angelica and glacé cherries to get more into the spirit of the time.

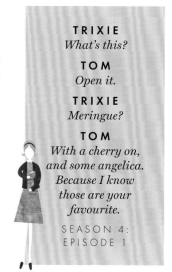

TRIXIE
What's this?

TOM
Open it.

TRIXIE
Meringue?

TOM
With a cherry on, and some angelica. Because I know those are your favourite.

SEASON 4:
EPISODE 1

COMMERCIAL CONFECTIONERY

The age of *Call the Midwife* was one in which sugar consumption boomed. In the home, sugar went into cakes and sweets, into tea and coffee, and onto porridge and breakfast cereal. Out of the home, it was in baked goods, drinks, and a vast and increasing range of branded sweets and chocolates. From Phyllis Crane's love of barley sugars to the Christmas edition box of Quality Street chocolates, we see the way in which confectionery was woven into everyday life for all classes at the time.

Sweets and chocolate had both been rationed until 1953, and in the first few years after this, people made up for lost time. Chocolate consumption rose by 26 percent over the 1930s, while that of sugar-based sweets rose by 16 percent. The frenzy peaked in the late 1950s, with chocolate consumption at 13 pounds (5.8 kg) and sweets at 14 pounds (6.3 kg) per person per annum. To put those numbers into appropriate perspective, that's about the weight of a three-month-old baby in each case. After that, people started to eat fewer sweets, though chocolate remained very popular and indeed consumption increased by the end of the 1960s.

Many of the sweets people ate weren't big brands. In Buckle's newsagent, we see sweeties from bulk jars lined up to be weighed, and that's the way most children—and many adults—bought confectionery. Favorites included bullseyes and humbugs, acid drops and toffees. In 1955, the first television ads for confectionery appeared, backed by large companies with the money to employ stars to endorse their products and to film the results. TV advertising was one of the biggest factors in changing the way people shopped and what they shopped for, and this was especially true of sweets. Milkybar, for example, launched in 1936, didn't start to take off until 1961, when the Milkybar kid first appeared on television. By 1972, it was one of Nestlé's biggest confectionery lines.

Along with everyday treats, the more special end of the market also continued to do well. The gift-worthy "fancy boxes" of the interwar years were now available as established names—Milk Tray, Black Magic, Dairy Box—while Rowntree's Quality Street vied with Cadbury's Roses for the family Christmas trade.

REGGIE
Are they for Collette?

NANCY
Liquorice Allsorts, her absolute favourite.

SEASON 11: EPISODE 7

A quick look at Britain's top twenty sweets for 1966 is illuminating. Mars Bar and Dairy Milk top the chart, with Wrigley's Spearmint third. Lower down are various mints, flavored chocolate bars, small packet sweets such as Smarties and Rolos, and chewy fruity things, including fruit gums, pastilles, and the now-forgotten Spangles (and Opal Fruits—aka Starburst in the twenty-first century). Most still exist, though the British companies that once made them have been bought out by multinationals. However, if you're looking to re-create the 1960s in confectionery form, be warned: Modern commercial pressure and tighter food regulations mean many have changed beyond all recognition. Maybe stick to cake instead.

CHERRY SLAB

Glacé cherries were quite a theme in the 1950s and 1960s. Candied cherries were nothing new, but the bright red type had been around for only a few decades. They can be divisive, as can their cousins, the cocktail cherry (maraschino cherry in the States). As far back as 1911, the New York Times *lamented that the treatment process took something nice—a fresh cherry—and rendered it "a tasteless indigestible thing . . . toughened and reduced to the semblance of a formless, gummy lump." However, they are sweet, bright, and jolly and remain well loved by many. This cake makes full use of them. It's typical of the simple, economical recipes found in many books from the mid-twentieth century: a very basic sponge with fruit added that is baked in a rectangular pan, which makes it easy to slice and store. Even the name is no-nonsense.*

SERVES 8–10

Preheat the oven to 325°F (165°C). Butter the bottom and sides of a 9×5-inch (23×13-cm) loaf pan, then line the bottom with parchment paper.

Sift together the flour and baking powder into a bowl. In a large bowl, using an electric mixer, beat together the butter and sugar on medium speed until the mixture is light in color and fluffy. Add the eggs, one at a time, along with a tablespoon of the flour mixture with each egg to prevent the mixture from curdling, beating well after each addition. On low speed, beat in the flour mixture along with the milk to form a smooth, pourable batter. Mix in the almonds.

Pour one-third of the batter into the pan and stud the batter with half of the cherries. Pour in another one-third of the batter and stud it with the remaining cherries. The cherries will probably still sink, but layering them this way gives them a fighting chance. Top with the remaining batter, smooth the top, and give the pan a couple of taps on the countertop to remove any air bubbles.

Bake the cake until a skewer inserted into the center comes out clean, 1–1½ hours. If the top begins to brown too much before the cake is ready, cover it loosely with aluminum foil. Let cool in the pan on a wire rack to room temperature, then turn it out onto the rack and peel off the parchment.

There's no need to decorate this cake. It's intended to be a very simple loaf cake for slicing up with a nice cup of tea.

RECIPE NOTE This cake can also be baked in a 10×2¼-inch (25×5.7-cm) deep-dish pie dish. Start checking the cake for doneness after about 45 minutes.

1 cup (225 g) butter, at room temperature, plus more for the pan

1¾ cups plus 1 tablespoon (225 g) flour

1 teaspoon baking powder

1 cup plus 1 tablespoon (225 g) superfine sugar

3 eggs

Finely grated zest of 1 lemon

3–4 tablespoons (45–60 ml) milk

½ cup (55 g) ground almonds

½ lb (225 g) glacé cherries

SISTER JULIENNE
Mrs. B made you a cherry slab as well, but Sister Monica Joan chose to spare it the journey.
SEASON 2: EPISODE 8

RUM BABA

Babas have a murky history. The name comes from Slavic linguistic traditions, where baba *or* babka *means "old lady" or "grandmother," and many babas are said to resemble the tall conical skirts that were in fashion in Europe for many centuries. In the twelfth century, babas were part of a tradition of yeast-risen cakes and breads that was Europe-wide but particularly rich in what is now Eastern Europe. However, the brioche-like modern confection seems to have developed later, probably in the sixteenth century. The innovation came about as a result of chefs in France playing with what was originally a plain fortified bread associated with Poland and Ukraine. By the 1930s, the baba had reached England and been translated as rum baba. In the 1950s, it was fast becoming a highly sought-after dessert, especially in restaurants, for it could be made in advance and left to soak. This recipe is based on one in* The Constance Spry Cookery Book, *published in 1956. Spry was a society florist turned cookery writer (she wrote in partnership with chef Rosemary Hume). On several occasions, Trixie refers to her training with Spry at her floristry school in Berkshire.*

SERVES 6–8

Start by combining the currants and 2 tablespoons rum in a small bowl and let soak for at least 4 hours but preferably overnight. If you forget to soak the currants, heat the rum to the boiling point, pour it over the fruit, and let steep for 30 minutes.

To make the sponge for the baba, in a bowl, combine the milk, superfine sugar, yeast, and 2–3 tablespoons of the flour, and stir together with a wooden spoon to make a thick paste. Set aside, uncovered, for 30 minutes.

Put the remaining flour, the salt, and eggs into the bowl of a stand mixer fitted with the dough hook, then add the sponge. Turn the mixer on low speed and mix for 1–2 minutes until the ingredients come together. Then increase the speed to medium-low and knead the dough until it is smooth and supple, 10–15 minutes.

Remove the bowl from the mixer stand and cover it with a damp kitchen towel or a reusable plastic cover. Let the dough rise in a warm, draft-free spot until doubled in size, 1–1½ hours.

Now return the bowl to the mixer stand. On medium-low speed, add the butter in a few batches, mixing well after each addition until fully incorporated before adding more. Finally, add the rum-soaked currants and mix until evenly distributed.

⅓ cup (55 g) dried currants

2 tablespoons rum

FOR THE BABA

¼ cup (60 ml) milk, warmed (100°–110°F/40°–43°C)

1 tablespoon superfine sugar

1 teaspoon active dried yeast

1⅔ cups (200 g) bread flour

Pinch of salt

2 eggs

6 tablespoons (90 g) butter, at room temperature, plus more for the pan

FOR THE SYRUP

2½ cups (600 ml) water

1½ cups (300 g) granulated sugar

1 vanilla bean

1 cup (240 ml) rum

TO FINISH

Sweetened whipped cream (from about 1 cup/240 ml heavy cream), for filling the center of the baba

At least 1 fl oz (30 ml) rum per serving, for individual shots

Recipe continues on the following page

Continued from the previous page

Butter a 9½-inch (24-cm) savarin mold or other ring-shape cake mold and transfer the dough to it. The mold should be no more than two-thirds full (the dough will be quite sloppy, so you may find a piping bag helpful). Cover with the damp towel or plastic cover, and let the dough rise in a warm, draft-free spot until it fills the mold, about 30 minutes. About 15 minutes before the dough is ready, preheat the oven to 350°F (180°C).

Bake the baba until it is golden brown, 30–40 minutes. Turn it out of the mold onto a wire rack and let cool completely. It is best if the baba is left for a day or so before soaking it in the syrup, but it can also be soaked on the day it is baked.

To make the syrup, in a saucepan, combine the water and granulated sugar over medium heat and heat, stirring occasionally, until the sugar dissolves. While the mixture is heating, using a paring knife, split the vanilla bean pod in half lengthwise and, using the tip of the knife, scrape the seeds from the pod halves. When the sugar syrup is ready, add the vanilla seeds and remove from the heat. Let the syrup cool, then stir in the rum.

When you are ready to soak your baba, simply immerse it in the syrup and leave it for 2–3 hours until it has soaked up lots of liquid. Then carefully slide the baba onto a serving plate and fill the center with the whipped cream. Pour any remaining syrup into a jug and offer at the table as an optional sauce. Then, for a final flourish, serve a shot of rum to everybody, which they can either pour over their slice of baba or drink.

RECIPE NOTE You can also make individual babas with this dough, using either tall-sided dariole molds or individual ring cake molds. In that case, reduce the baking time to 20–30 minutes. The number of molds you need will vary depending on their size. Remember to fill them two-thirds full for the second rise. If you aren't keen on dried fruit, simply leave out the currants. You can also serve babas with fresh fruit—strawberries are ideal—but don't go overboard.

NURSE CRANE
Coconut sandwich, date and walnut loaf, fruit scones with butter, plain scones with jam, rum baba, Swiss roll, macaroons!

TRIXIE
Is this the refreshment menu for the mannequin parade?

NURSE CRANE
No. It's all the varieties of cake that Sister Monica Joan has refused in the last six weeks. I've taken to making notes.

SEASON 10: EPISODE 1

LIGHT GINGER CAKE

Ginger turns up in quite a few concoctions in Call the Midwife, *from port and ginger down the Cock and Bull to the ginger nut biscuits consumed with enthusiasm by Nonnatus residents and their patients alike. Gingery things are recommended for nausea, including morning sickness, and ginger is well known as a stomach settler. If you want something more biscuit-like, try the gingerbread figures on page 73. However, if you are in the mood for cake, this is excellent. It is lighter than traditional parkin-style gingerbreads, which are made with oats and black treacle, while still retaining the sticky spiciness so characteristic of this type of cake. It also keeps well, which is good news for those who say that gingerbread should be kept for at least three days before eating. That also means you can make the cake a few days in advance and decorate it at your leisure. The decoration is a scheme suggested by quite a lot of writers of the time, and while it takes some time, it does look fabulous.*

SERVES 8–10

To make the cake, preheat the oven to 300°F (150°C). Liberally butter a 12×8-inch (30×20-cm) pan.

Sift together the flour, ground ginger, and mixed spice into the bowl of a stand mixer fitted with the paddle attachment (or a large bowl if using a handheld mixer). In a small saucepan, combine the butter, golden syrup, stem ginger syrup, and granulated sugar over low heat, and heat just until the butter melts and the sugar dissolves. Remove from the heat. Crack the eggs into a medium bowl. In a small bowl, dissolve the baking soda in the milk, and add the milk to the butter mixture. Pour the contents of the saucepan onto the eggs while whisking constantly to mix well. Now pour the liquid ingredients into the flour mixture and beat on medium speed until all the ingredients are incorporated and you have a smooth batter. Mix in the chopped ginger. Transfer the batter to the prepared pan.

Bake the cake until springy to the touch and a skewer inserted into the center comes out clean, 45–60 minutes. Let cool in the pan on a wire rack for 20–30 minutes, then turn the cake out onto the rack, turn upright, and let cool completely.

To finish the cake, first make a simple glacé icing by sifting the confectioners' sugar into a bowl and then stirring in the lemon juice and enough syrup to make a stiff, spreadable icing. Place the cake on a serving plate and, using a palette knife or an offset spatula, spread the icing evenly over the top. Slice the stem ginger very thinly. Arrange the pieces on the icing, either overlapping them (like fish scales) or laying them in a checkerboard pattern. Obviously, you can use a few silver balls for good measure.

FOR THE CAKE

½ cup (115 g) butter, plus more for the pan

2¼ cups (280 g) flour

2 teaspoons ground ginger

1 teaspoon mixed spice

½ cup (170 g) golden syrup

¼ cup (60 ml) syrup from stem ginger in syrup

6½ tablespoons (85 g) granulated sugar

2 eggs

1 teaspoon baking soda

6 tablespoons (90 ml) milk

2 tablespoons drained, chopped stem ginger in syrup

TO FINISH

1¾ cups (225 g) confectioners' sugar

1 teaspoon fresh lemon juice

2–3 tablespoons syrup from jarred stem ginger in syrup

Rest of jar of stem ginger, drained (9–10 oz/250–285 g)

Silver balls (optional)

APPLESAUCE CAKE

A version of this recipe, for a cake more common in the United States than in Britain, features in Peggy Hutchinson's delightfully snippy Home Made Cake, Pastry and Biscuit Secrets, *published in the mid-1950s. It's based on the 1-2-3-4 cake principle, building up the butter, sugar, and flour proportionately and replacing half of the eggs with applesauce. Apples feature several times as an ingredient in* Call the Midwife, *which, despite its urban setting, reminds us that fruits and vegetables are seasonal. Fred's allotment is a constant source of vegetables, while grateful parents regularly offer produce from their own plots and gardens to the nuns and nurses at Nonnatus House. This can get to be too much. In season 5, episode 5, we see the Nonnatus residents become progressively less keen on the produce rolling around on the porch. This recipe uses only two cooking apples, but it's a start.*

SERVES 10–12

To make the applesauce, in a saucepan, combine the apples and wine over medium-high heat and bring to a boil. Reduce the heat to a simmer and cook, stirring occasionally, until the apples break down and are very soft, about 15 minutes. Remove from the heat and, using a potato masher or spoon, mash to a smooth purée. Measure 1 cup (255 g) for the cake and set aside to cool. Reserve any remaining applesauce for another use. You can do this stage in advance.

To make the cake, preheat the oven to 350°F (180°C). Butter the bottom and sides of 10×8-inch (26×20-cm) baking pan or dish.

In a medium bowl, combine the flour, cinnamon, nutmeg, baking powder, and baking soda and stir to mix. In a large bowl, using an electric mixer, beat together the butter and superfine sugar on medium speed until the mixture is light in color and fluffy. Add the eggs, one at a time, along with a tablespoon of the flour mixture with each egg to prevent the mixture from curdling, beating well after each addition. Once the eggs are thoroughly incorporated, add the applesauce and beat until blended. On low speed, add the remaining flour mixture and dates and/or raisins, and beat just until well mixed. Transfer the batter to the prepared pan and smooth the top.

Bake the cake until a skewer inserted into the center comes out clean, 35–40 minutes. Let the cake cool completely in the pan on a wire rack before serving. The cake can be served plain or with a dusting of confectioners' sugar on top.

RECIPE NOTE You can use store-bought applesauce for this cake, in which case add ½ teaspoon ground ginger to it before using. If making the applesauce, a Bramley apple (the best-known UK cooking apple) is ideal. You need an apple that will fall apart and fluff up when cooked. You could also use a dual-purpose apple, such as a James Grieve or even the russets and Worcesters that we see being carefully wrapped for storage at Nonnatus House in season 5. In the United States, McIntosh and Golden Delicious are good choices for applesauce.

FOR THE APPLESAUCE

2 cooking apples (see Recipe Note), peeled, cored, and diced

¼ cup (60 ml) ginger wine

FOR THE CAKE

6 tablespoons (90 g) butter, at room temperature, plus more for the pan

2¾ cups (340 g) flour

1 teaspoon ground cinnamon

½ teaspoon ground nutmeg

1½ teaspoons baking powder

¾ teaspoon baking soda

1 cup plus 2 tablespoons (225 g) superfine sugar

2 eggs

1 cup (255 g) applesauce (above)

¾ cup (125 g) chopped dates or golden raisins, or a mixture

1–2 tablespoons confectioners' sugar, for dusting (optional)

HALF-A-POUND CAKE (BIRTHDAY CAKE)

Birthdays in Call the Midwife *aren't always remarked upon. However, when they are, there's often cake (much to Sister Monica Joan's delight). The Turners' children have a particularly excellent set of annual cakes, often iced in blue, which was only available as a stable food dye from the 1930s and rapidly became unnervingly popular. This recipe is a basic one, a cut-down version of the venerable pound cake, so-called because it used a pound (450 g) of every ingredient. The pound cake was first mentioned in print in 1743 and spread to America with the introduction of English-authored cookery books around the same time. You can simply cover the cake with fondant and pipe "Happy Birthday" on top, as seen in the show. The presentation here is one suggested by both* Good Housekeeping *and* Woman's Realm *magazines in the 1950s. It's an ideal bake for two working parents trying to get a birthday tea on the table when the maternity hospital they work at is a little short-staffed.*

SERVES 8–10

To make the cake, preheat the oven to 350°F (180°C). Butter the bottom and sides of a 7-inch (18-cm) round springform pan, then line the bottom with parchment paper.

Sift together the flour and baking powder into a medium bowl. In a large bowl, using an electric mixer, beat together the butter and superfine sugar on medium speed until light in color and fluffy. Add the eggs, one at a time, along with a tablespoon of the flour mixture with each egg to prevent the mixture from curdling, beating well after each addition. On low speed, add the remaining flour mixture and beat until well mixed. Pour the batter into the prepared pan and make a slight hollow in the center so the top will be flat when the cake comes out of the oven.

Bake the cake until the top is golden brown and a skewer inserted into the center comes out clean, about 20 minutes. Let cool in the pan on a wire rack for 5 minutes, then unclasp and lift off the pan sides, invert the cake onto the rack, lift off the pan bottom, and peel off the parchment. Turn the cake upright on the rack and let cool completely.

When you are ready to decorate, start by coloring the marzipan with cocoa powder. Place the marzipan on a work surface and, if necessary, knead it gently until it is pliable. Sprinkle it with 1 tablespoon of the cocoa powder and knead in the powder until the marzipan is evenly colored, adding more cocoa powder as needed to achieve the shade of brown you like.

FOR THE CAKE

1 cup (225 g) butter, at room temperature, plus more for the pan

1¾ cups plus 1 tablespoon (225 g) flour

2 teaspoons baking powder

1 cup plus 2 tablespoons (225 g) superfine sugar

4 eggs

2 teaspoons pure vanilla extract

TO DECORATE

About ¼ lb (115 g) marzipan, at room temperature

1–2 tablespoons unsweetened cocoa powder, plus more for the work surface

1¾ cups (225 g) confectioners' sugar

2 tablespoons boiling water, cooled

Crystallized violets, glacé cherries, candied angelica, candles, and silver balls (optional)

Recipe continues on the following page

Continued from the previous page

Lightly dust a work surface with cocoa powder and top with the marzipan. Roll out the marzipan about ¼ inch (6 mm) thick. Using a small rabbit-shape cookie cutter (no taller than the cake), cut out 6–8 rabbit shapes. Next, if you have a set of small number-shape cookie cutters (0–9), cut out the numbers you will need for a clock face. If you don't have number-shape cutters, you can make roman numerals with a few simple cuts. Finally, cut out two clock hands. Set aside all the cutouts to harden.

Now make a glacé icing. Sift the confectioners' sugar into a bowl. Gradually add the boiling water while constantly mixing well until you have a very thick mixture that slowly spreads outward if you pull the spoon through it.

Stand the wire rack with the cake on it on a sheet pan to catch any drips. Pour the icing onto the center of the cake, covering the top completely and allowing the icing to drip down the sides to cover them too. If necessary, use a rubber spatula to ensure the sides are completely covered.

Allow the icing to dry slightly, but before it completely sets, stick the rabbits around the sides of the cake and make a clock face on top with the numbers and hands. The original guidance is to use the hands to show the child's age. If you like, use the crystallized flowers, glacé cherries, and angelica to form a vague garden around the rabbits and add candles and silver balls as desired. You can also pipe the child's name on the cake—why not?

FOOD FACT Trompe l'oeil foods are as old as cuisine itself, but novelty cakes date to the late nineteenth century, when sugar became cheap (due mainly to the switch from cane to beet sugar, as well as to a drop in duty on imports) and tin molds were mass-produced. By the 1920s, they were being promoted as children's cakes, with designs that included the princess or "a lady" cake (the one with the doll stuck in the middle and a cake hooped skirt). In the 1960s, they boomed, and it became a mark of pride and skill to turn out an iced train, book, or sweet-encrusted house for a child's birthday party.

VALERIE
Sister, is Sister Julienne really not going to let Sister Monica Joan have a little birthday celebration?

SISTER WINIFRED
I'm sure the order would run to a sponge cake with a candle on it. But she's just not allowed to receive presents. They'd count as personal possessions.

SEASON 7:
EPISODE 8

MALT LOAF

Advances in food chemistry at the end of the nineteenth century, along with a brief vogue for malt as a health supplement, led to the invention of malt extract, a treacle-like substance that formed the basis for a range of products, including drinks, jellies (gelatin desserts), and bread. Malt bread, now known mainly as malt loaf, became a popular teatime accompaniment, not least as it kept very well and was very dense, making it ideal for toting in a pocket. By the 1950s, it was a commercial product and rarely made at home. It would have been sold at both the bread stalls we see in the Poplar market and the many bakeries that then still lined the streets. In season 2, episode 6, we glimpse the hard work behind the scenes at such bakeries, which relied on nighttime working and were often only partially mechanized.

Malt bread is best served slathered in salted butter, but it is also excellent with a slab of cheese. You can serve it as is or toast it, but be careful if you decide to toast it, as the level of sugars it contains means it can burn quite easily.

SERVES 8–10

The dough for this loaf can be made by hand or with a stand mixer. Put both flours into a large bowl or into the bowl of a stand mixer and stir briefly to mix. Make a well in the center of the flour mixture. Pour half of the water into the well, sprinkle in the yeast and sugar, and then sprinkle some flour from the sides of the well on top. Leave until the yeast starts to bubble through the flour layer, 10–15 minutes.

In a small saucepan, combine the treacle, golden syrup, and malt extract over low heat and heat until the mixture liquefies, then add the butter, which will melt. Remove from the heat, add the remaining water to the pan, and then stir in the fruit. (This makes it easier to pour.) Add this mixture to the flour-yeast mixture along with the salt and mix well. If mixing by hand, mix with a wooden spoon. If using a stand mixer, fit the mixer with the dough hook, turn the mixer on low speed, and mix for 1–2 minutes until the ingredients come together.

Knead the dough in the bowl for about 20 minutes by hand or for about 10 minutes on medium-low speed in the stand mixer (this latter is much easier as the dough will be quite wet). The dough is ready when it forms a lump at the bottom of the bowl that is tacky to the touch but not too wet. Remove the bowl from the mixer stand, if used. Cover the bowl with a damp kitchen towel or a reusable plastic cover and let the dough rise in a warm, draft-free spot until it has roughly doubled in size, about 1½ hours.

1¾ cups plus 1 tablespoon (225 g) bread flour

1¾ cups plus 1 tablespoon (225 g) whole wheat flour

1 cup (240 ml) tepid water (100°–110°F/40°–43°C)

2 teaspoons active dry yeast

1 teaspoon brown sugar

1½ tablespoons black treacle

1½ teaspoons golden syrup

3 tablespoons malt extract

2 tablespoons butter, plus more for the pan

¾ cup (125 g) mixed golden raisins and chopped prunes

1 teaspoon salt

Butter a 9×5-inch (23×12-cm) loaf pan. Shape the dough gently to fit and place it in the prepared pan. Cover with the damp towel or plastic cover and let the dough rise in a warm, draft-free spot for about 1 hour. It should rise to fill the pan. About 15 minutes before the dough is ready, preheat the oven to 400°F (200°C).

Bake the bread until lightly golden, 50–60 minutes. Let cool in the pan on a wire rack to room temperature before turning out. Wrap the cooled loaf in parchment paper or a clean cloth (not in a sealed plastic container) and store at room temperature for at least 3 days or up to 1 week to mature before eating.

FOOD FACT Many of the cakes and other baked goods we see in the series come from Dunns Bakery in Crouch End in North London. In season 10, the bakery supplied Lucille's wedding cake. The family has been baking bread and other such goodies since 1820, and the bakery is a rare survivor in an industry that now relies on mass-manufacturing and supermarket distribution. Happily, good bread is having a resurgence and, with it, good bakeries.

CYNTHIA
Has anyone else noticed a button's come off his clinical coat? He's got no one to sew it on for him.

TRIXIE
It hardly inspires confidence! Ugh, and his poor little boy's looking quite unkempt.

SISTER BERNADETTE
Speak more respectfully of Doctor, please. And I'll thank you to hand me the malt loaf.

SEASON 2:
EPISODE 1

SMALL CAKES AND BISCUITS

SERGEANT WOOLF

Er . . . generally it's the cakes one hears about whenever Nonnatus House is discussed among the members of the Constabulary.

SEASON 8: EPISODE 1

COCONUT MACAROONS

Coconut was a very popular flavoring in the 1950s, whether in large layer cakes, like the one on page 15, or in smaller confections. Coconut macaroons were enjoyed for both their light color and delicate flavor. We hear of macaroons several times in Call the Midwife. *Usually, they are plain almond ones, but cherry macaroons (almond macaroons with a cherry on top) appear in season 8 when Sister Monica Joan is matchmaking between Lucille and Cyril. For a conventional macaroon recipe, see the Sherry Cake on page 21. This version is more like a rock cake—another 1960s staple. They are very good plain, but you can give them a basic icing glaze, if you like.*

MAKES 20 MACAROONS

Preheat the oven to 425°F (220°C). Line a large sheet pan (or two smaller sheet pans) with parchment paper or a silicone baking mat.

In a large bowl, combine the flour, baking powder, sugar, and coconut, and stir to mix. Scatter the butter over the flour mixture and, using your fingers, work in the butter until well mixed. Add the egg and stir to mix. Then, while continuing to stir, gradually add the milk, using just enough to slacken the mixture, making a workable dough. It should be pretty stiff.

Divide the dough into 20 equal portions and arrange them about 2 inches (5 cm) apart on the prepared sheet pan. Top each one with half of a glacé cherry.

Bake the macaroons until they begin to brown, 12–15 minutes. Let cool completely on the pan on a wire rack before serving.

1²/₃ cups (200 g) flour

1 teaspoon baking powder

³/₄ cup (150 g) sugar

1¹/₃ cups (110 g) unsweetened shredded dried coconut

6 tablespoons (90 g) butter, cut into small cubes

1 egg, lightly beaten

5–6 tablespoons (75–90 ml) milk

5 glacé cherries, halved

1960s SPIN *Coconut sometimes inspired some gloriously wacky designs. The Spalding Guardian published a recipe for "angel cakes" in 1968, which were made from sweetened condensed milk mixed with enough shredded coconut to make a stiff batter. This was divided up and formed into cones for bodies and balls for heads, which were then duly stuck together and baked (at 325°F/165°C for 3–5 minutes if you fancy trying it). The enterprising cook was instructed to make halos and wings from silver foil, though how they were affixed was left a mystery. Being 1968, some of the angels were also colored red and blue.*

SISTER EVANGELINA
Are we gonna get that tea in the clinical room or aren't we?

SISTER WINIFRED
Oh, I'm sorry. I had a problem with the desiccated coconut.

SISTER EVANGELINA
Oh, if we have to wait much longer, you'll have a problem with a desiccated corpse. Mine!

SEASON 5: CHRISTMAS

FAIRY CAKES

A classic presentation of a simple small cake, butterfly cakes appear at the Turners' children's birthday parties as well as raising a smile at fundraising events and other public parties. They aren't sophisticated, but they are very sweet. The basic cake is also known as a fairy cake— so-called as it is a light sponge—and the butterfly part comes from the way it is decorated, with the peaked top removed, divided in two, and replaced to look like a butterfly's wings. The cakes became popular between the wars, though have since declined somewhat faced with competition from the rather more brutish American-style cupcakes and muffins. Fairy cakes are significantly smaller than cupcakes, so be careful with your choice of pan. In the United Kingdom, you can buy fairy cake pans, which are very shallow. If you do not have one, then a standard muffin pan lined with suitably sized paper liners should be fine, but be careful not to overfill the cups. Think gently fluttering peacock butterfly, not a galumphing giant swallowtail.

If you are making plain fairy cakes, they should never be adulterated with buttercream or frosting. Basic glacé icing is all you need. However, if you opt for the butterfly version and you aren't used to using glacé icing, whipped cream is better for keeping the wings in place.

MAKES 12 SMALL CAKES

To make the cakes, preheat the oven to 350°F (180°C). Line 12 standard fairy cake cups with paper liners.

Sift together the flour, baking powder, and salt into a medium bowl. In a large bowl, using an electric mixer, beat together the butter and superfine sugar on medium speed until the mixture is light in color and fluffy. Add the vanilla, if using, and mix until blended. Add the eggs, one at a time, along with a tablespoon of the flour mixture with each egg to prevent the mixture from curdling, beating well after each addition. On low speed, gradually add the flour mixture, mixing just until incorporated.

Spoon the batter into the prepared cups, dividing it evenly. Bake until golden and a toothpick inserted into the center of a cake or two comes out clean, 15–20 minutes. Let cool completely in the pan on a wire rack, then remove from the pan.

When you are ready to decorate the cakes, choose whether you wish to make fairy cakes or butterfly cakes (or both).

For fairy cakes, make a simple glacé icing by sifting the confectioners' sugar into a bowl and then stirring in the lemon juice and enough water to make a nice icing consistency. It can be fairly runny. Just layer a few teaspoons of the icing atop each cake, allow it to set slightly, and then go large with the silver balls.

FOR THE CAKES

1½ cups (185 g) flour

1 teaspoon baking powder

Pinch of salt

¾ cup (170 g) butter, at room temperature

¾ cup (150 g) superfine sugar

2 teaspoons pure vanilla extract (optional)

3 eggs

FOR FAIRY CAKES

1⅔ cups (200 g) confectioners' sugar

1 teaspoon fresh lemon juice

1–2 tablespoons warm water

Silver balls or hundreds and thousands, for decorating

FOR BUTTERFLY CAKES

¾ cup (180 ml) heavy cream

Confectioners' sugar, for dusting

Recipe continues on the following page

Continued from the previous page

For butterfly cakes, cut the peaked top off of each cake and divide it in two. In a bowl, whisk the cream by hand or with a handheld mixer on medium-high speed until stiff peaks form. Spoon (or pipe) some of the whipped cream onto the center of each cake. Use the cream to stick the halves of the cake back onto the top, placing them to resemble wings. Dust the cakes lightly with confectioners' sugar.

SISTER JULIENNE
Is that a butterfly cake?

SISTER WINIFRED
Yes! Erm Mrs. Turner sent some after Angela's party.

SEASON 7: EPISODE 8

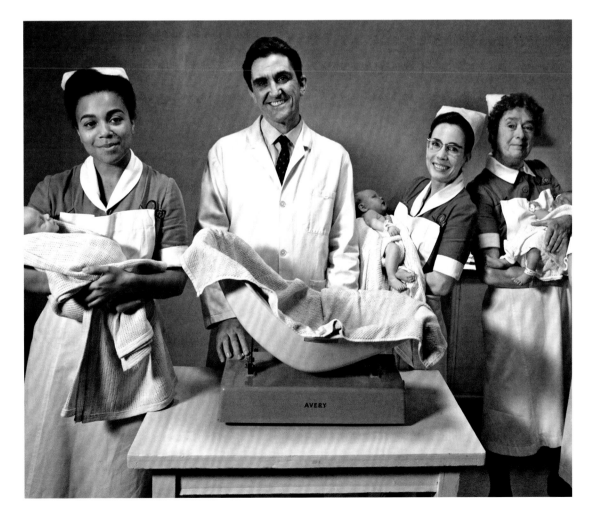

CHOCOLATE KRACKOLATES

Breakfast cereals were introduced to Britain between the wars but were slow to catch on. As one food writer harrumphed, "No one who can get good porridge would want to eat those nauseating American proprietary cereals." However, the dual pressures of convenience and American glamour meant that by the time Call the Midwife *opens in 1956, cereals were becoming ever more common. From Chummy's bran flakes to the quasi-ubiquitous cornflakes, the bright branding of cereal packets feature in many a Poplar home in the series. But they weren't just a feature of breakfast: This ridiculously simple no-cook recipe was actively promoted by Kellogg's and was a favorite to make with children. The original Kellogg's pamphlet calls the Rice Krispies version chocolate krispies, while the cornflakes one was krackolates, a name that surely deserves a revival.*

MAKES 8–12 INDIVIDUAL TREATS

Have ready 8–12 paper liners for a fairy cake pan or a muffin pan, arranging them on a sheet pan or a tray, or line a large sheet pan with parchment paper or a silicone baking mat.

Put the chocolate into a large heatproof bowl, place over (not touching) simmering water in a saucepan, and heat, stirring occasionally, until melted and smooth (or melt in a microwave). Remove from over the water; add the butter, golden syrup, and orange zest (if using), and stir to mix. Now fold in the cornflakes and mix gently until they are evenly coated with the chocolate mixture.

Spoon the cornflakes mixture into the paper cups or dollop 8–12 neat heaps of the mixture onto the prepared sheet pan. Sprinkle each treat with hundreds and thousands, and put them in the fridge for at least 1 hour to set before serving.

3 oz (90 g) milk chocolate

2 tablespoons butter

2 tablespoons golden syrup

2 teaspoons finely grated orange zest (optional)

2⅓ cups (75 g) lightly crushed cornflakes or whole Rice Krispies

Hundreds and thousands, for decorating

SISTER JULIENNE
You're fully dilated now, Glenys, and you can push as hard as you like on the next pain.

GLENYS
Oh, am I going to have it here?

SISTER JULIENNE
Yes, you are.

GLENYS
Oh, I can see Rice Krispies on the lino!

SEASON 10: EPISODE 1

SCONES

Scones are a classic of the British tea table, though as a baking powder–leavened dough, they are a relative newcomer to the culinary repertoire. Baking powder was invented in the mid-nineteenth century and didn't become universal in scone recipes until the early twentieth century. Before then, scones were made with yeast and had a strong Scottish association. However, the rise of afternoon tea in the late nineteenth century, and more particularly the growth in motorcar-based tourism from the 1920s onward, meant that tearooms with an eye to the tourist trade wanted cheap, easy goods to sell to hungry motorists. Scones are quick to make and neutral enough that they can easily be given a flavorsome individual twist, ideal for busy catering operations. They became popular in homes as well, and we see them in Call the Midwife *at such occasions as the various street parties and being served with tea at Nonnatus House. They would have been an ideal accompaniment for Violet Buckle's infamously excellent jam.*

MAKES 6 SCONES

Preheat the oven to 425°F (220°C). Have ready an ungreased sheet pan.

In a large bowl, whisk together the flour, baking powder, granulated sugar, and salt. Using a large spoon, stir in the cream just until evenly moistened. Using your hands, gently gather the dough together, kneading it against the side of the bowl until it holds together in a rough ball.

Lightly flour a work surface and turn the dough out onto it. Roll out the dough about ¾ inch (2 cm) thick. Using a 3-inch (7.5-cm) round cutter, cut out rounds from the dough, pressing straight down and lifting straight up and cutting them as closely together as possible. Place the dough rounds at least 2 inches (5 cm) apart on the sheet pan. Gather up the dough scraps, knead briefly on the floured work surface, roll out the dough again, cut out more rounds, and add them to the pan.

Using a pastry brush, lightly brush the tops of the scones with the sweetened milk.

Bake the scones until golden, 10–12 minutes. Transfer to a wire rack to cool. Serve warm or at room temperature.

RECIPE TIP For golden raisin scones, add ½ cup (70 g) golden raisins with the cream and proceed as directed in the recipe. For cheese scones, combine the dry ingredients as directed. Cut 4 tablespoons (60 g) cold butter into small cubes, scatter them over the flour mixture, and then, using your fingertips, work the butter into the flour mixture just until you have a crumbly mixture. Sprinkle 1 cup (115 g) grated sharp cheddar cheese over the butter-flour mixture and work it in with your fingertips just until evenly distributed. Substitute ⅓ cup plus 1 tablespoon (85 ml) milk for the cream, stirring it in just until the mixture is evenly moistened. Proceed as directed in the recipe.

2 cups (250 g) flour, plus more for the work surface

1 tablespoon baking powder

2 teaspoons granulated sugar

1 teaspoon salt

¾ cup plus 2 tablespoons (200 ml) heavy cream

TO FINISH

1½ tablespoons milk, sweetened with 1 teaspoon granulated sugar

CHUMMY
Mater would thoroughly approve of this. She always wanted me to slenderise. Then, when she was dying, she pushed a plate of scones towards me and said, "Camilla, look after your face. The other end's for sitting on, nobody will ever see it."

SEASON 4:
EPISODE 8

ICED BUNS

Iced buns are one of the staples of Call the Midwife, *eaten throughout all eleven seasons with great relish. Mainly they appear as the plain sort, essentially a sweetened white bread with fondant icing on top. Sometimes the very British Belgian bun features instead: the same dough filled with lemon curd and currants and rolled into a snail, then baked, iced, and always served with a glacé cherry on top. These buns were bakery goods, not made at home, and traditional British high street bakers still often have a display of them—they can reach quite enormous proportions—in the window or on a countertop. We first meet them in* Call the Midwife *when Jenny eats them for a quick burst of energy between deliveries, and all of the nurses at one time or another seem to unwrap the characteristic brown bag from the bakery. Sister Monica Joan gives one to Sister Ursula as she departs at the end of episode 3 of season 6—a typical act of kindness and forgiveness even when deep hurt has been caused.*

MAKES 13 BUNS (A BAKER'S DOZEN)

To make the buns, pour the lukewarm milk into a small bowl, sprinkle the yeast on top, and let stand until the yeast is softened, 5–10 minutes. Put both flours, the granulated sugar, and salt in the bowl of a stand mixer and stir to mix. Add the yeast mixture and eggs to the bowl and fit the mixer with the dough hook. Turn the mixer on low speed and mix for 1–2 minutes until the ingredients come together. Then gradually add the butter, beating until a smooth, relatively moist mixture forms, stopping to scrape down the sides of the bowl as needed. Increase the speed to medium-low and knead the dough until it is smooth and elastic, about 10 minutes.

Remove the bowl from the mixer stand and cover it with a damp kitchen towel or a reusable plastic cover. Let the dough rise in a warm, draft-free spot until doubled in size, 1–2 hours.

Line a large sheet pan with parchment paper or a silicone baking mat. Divide the dough into 13 equal portions. Roll each portion into a ball and then shape into a finger about 5 inches (13 cm) long. Arrange the dough fingers on the prepared sheet pan, leaving just enough space between for them to roughly double in size. Cover with a damp kitchen towel and let the buns rise in a warm, draft-free spot until they are puffed and lightly touching one another, about 45 minutes. About 15 minutes before the dough is ready, preheat the oven to 400°F (200°C).

Bake the buns until they are pale golden brown, 20–25 minutes. Transfer the buns to a wire rack and let cool completely.

FOR THE BUNS

1 cup (240 ml) milk, warmed
(100°–110°F/40°–43°C)

2 teaspoons active dried yeast

1¾ cups plus 1 tablespoon
(225 g) bread flour

1¾ cups plus 1 tablespoon
(225 g) flour

¼ cup (50 g) granulated sugar

1 teaspoon salt

2 eggs

6 tablespoons (90 g) butter,
at room temperature

FOR THE ICING

1⅔ cups (200 g)
confectioners' sugar

1 teaspoon fresh lemon juice

About 1 tablespoon warm water

Pink food coloring, preferably
in powder form (optional)

To make the icing, sift the confectioners' sugar into a bowl, then stir in the lemon juice and enough water to make a good piping consistency. Spoon the icing into a piping bag fitted with a medium plain tip. Alternatively, if desired, spoon half of the icing into a second bowl and mix in enough food coloring to turn it a pretty pink, then use two piping bags (or plastic bags with a corner snipped off), one for each color.

When the buns are cool, gently pull them apart. Pipe a thin, steady line of icing along the top of each bun, then, using a palette knife or an offset spatula, spread the icing to cover the top. Eat the buns the same day, as they go stale quickly.

RECIPE NOTE If you want to make these buns into Belgian buns, at the shaping stage, roll out the dough on a lightly floured work surface into a rectangle about 10×16 inches (25×40 cm). Spread the dough with a thin layer of lemon curd and sprinkle it with currants. Roll it up from the long side like a Swiss (jelly) roll and cut it crosswise into 13 pieces. Stand each piece on a cut side on the prepared pan, then cover with the towel or plastic cover and let rise for about 30 minutes. Bake as directed in the recipe. Ice the tops and put a glacé cherry on each one.

TRIXIE
Iced buns! Iced buns! Iced buns donated by a kindly baker. Tuck in. Working men get first pick!

JACK
Never mind working men. What about growing boys?

TRIXIE
Oh, the kindly baker sent some dry bread.

SEASON 3: CHRISTMAS

A GUIDE TO BISCUITS

Biscuits are an ancient and very ill-defined food. The name comes from the Latin for "twice cooked," and many early biscuits were exactly that: double baked, or boiled then baked. But they rapidly evolved, and the term now covers all sorts of things, from the ship's biscuits of the eighteenth century—so rock solid they were sometimes used as postcards—to wafers, waffles, macaroons, shortbreads, and sponge-type confections that veer very close to cake.

By the late nineteenth century, commercially manufactured biscuits were widely available, made by such companies as Peek Frean, Huntley & Palmers, McVitie's, and Carr's—companies whose names sometimes survive today but are all now owned by multinationals. However, they were behind a massive range of biscuits, many of which became household names, and many of which regularly appear on-screen in *Call the Midwife*.

By the 1950s, biscuits held a very special place in British hearts. They'd been derationed in 1949 (plain) and 1950 (sweet), and consumption stood at about 6 ounces (170 g) per person per week by 1958 (that's about twelve biscuits). During rationing, biscuits had been a cake substitute, boosting morale with a morsel of sweetness and helping watery tea taste just a little bit better. Now even the plainer biscuits carried connotations of joy, and the return of the luxurious filled dainties—Bourbons, Gypsy creams, custard creams, and the like—upped the ante even more. And although most of the varieties were prewar favorites, there were new arrivals, too, including the Jammie Dodger (jam-filled shortbread) in 1960.

Here, for the uninitiated, is a quick rundown of the most often seen biscuits in and around Nonnatus House.

Garibaldi: Also known as squashed fly cake and other similar names, the Garibaldi, which consists of two thin, rectangular biscuits sandwiching squished currants, is secretly rather lovely. Named for Giuseppe Garibaldi, who led the fight for the unification of Italy, the biscuits were first made by Peek Frean in 1861. Jenny and Alec bond over them in season 2.

Pink Wafer: Occupying the gray zone bridging biscuit, cake, and something that should be covered in chocolate, versions of these delicate sandwich biscuits were circulating in the late nineteenth century.

ALEC
Ah, biscuits? Marvellous.

JENNY
Garibaldi, I'm afraid.

ALEC
We used to call them "fly cemeteries" when we were kids.

JENNY
So did we! (they laugh) We were always pleased to see them, though. Any port in a storm during rationing.

SEASON 2: EPISODE 8

Both the wafers and the vanilla-flavor cream filling are pink, and Shelagh eats a whole packet when in labor with Teddy in season 6.

Gipsy Cream: A fairly short-lived McVitie's offering, this sandwich biscuit has a chocolate-flavor riff on the outside of both digestives and chocolate buttercream between them. Nurse Dyer stashed three packets in her luggage for the Outer Hebrides. Not to be confused with the custard cream, which has a custard-flavor filling and no chocolate.

Digestive: Originally marketed in the early nineteenth century to aid digestion, all health claims had been dropped for digestives by the 1950s. Made with whole-wheat and all-purpose flours, they are highly versatile, excellent with tea or with cheese. A chocolate version is also available.

Rich Tea: Much (and unfairly) maligned, including by Sergeant Woolf, these unadorned biscuits are on the shelves at Nonnatus House for emergency use. Plain they might be, but they are hard to better with a cup of tea.

Ginger Nut: Properly solid, treacle-sweetened ginger biscuits, ginger nuts were originally baked to resemble a nut (walnut size is a common instruction in nineteenth century cookery books). They are served at the bingo hall when Cyril and Lucille join Valerie and her gran in episode 7 of season 8.

Lemon Puff: Another sandwich biscuit, this one layers a lemon filling between two light, flaky biscuits. More popular today in Sri Lanka than in Britain, lemon puffs are an excellent demonstration that the effects of empire weren't just to alter British tastes but also affect the nations the British colonized. Sister Monica Joan is particularly partial to them.

Bourbon: Launched as Creola in 1910, with a name change about two decades later to introduce a hint of royalty to the proceedings (Bourbon is the name of the deposed French royal family), these rectangular chocolate sandwich biscuits with a chocolate filling are one of the posher of the everyday biscuits.

SHORTBREAD

Shortbread is more often seen than commented on in Call the Midwife. *There's usually a plate of it lurking by the telephone. It takes various forms and is especially prevalent at Christmas. In the season 2 Christmas special, as Trixie tries to coax Sister Monica Joan's hyacinths into life, she's aided by petticoat tails donated by a grateful patient. In season 10, the Turner children make shortbread in the shape of nurses. We also see it in more everyday rectangular blocks.*

Shortbread has strong Scottish links, emerging out of the sixteenth century shift toward butter-based cuisine among the rich, and is dependent on white flour, which was a way to distinguish the cuisine of the wealthy from that of the more generally oat-based dishes of the majority of the population of Scotland and northern England. Early recipes often included candied peel, ground almonds, or caraway seeds. By the twentieth century, it was usual to add a bit of rice flour to guarantee a good crisp crack. Make sure the butter you use here is top-quality salted.

MAKES 16–20 SMALL BISCUITS OR 8 LARGE PETTICOAT TAILS

Preheat the oven to 325°F (165°C). Line a sheet pan with parchment paper or a silicone baking mat.

Sift together both flours and the sugar into a bowl. Scatter the butter pieces over the flour mixture and, using a pastry blender or your fingertips, work the butter into the flour mixture until a crumbly mixture forms. Knead the mixture in the bowl just until it comes together in a ball. To make large triangular petticoat tails, transfer the dough to the center of the prepared sheet pan and flatten it into a thick disk. Roll out the dough very gently directly into a circle 9 inches (23 cm) in diameter and just under ½ inch (12 mm) thick. (Topping it with a sheet of parchment paper or a silicone baking mat helps to prevent it from sticking to the rolling pin.) You can use a tart ring or cake pan as a guide. Crimp the edges with your fingers to form scallops. Chill the dough for 15 to 20 minutes, then lightly prick it all over with a fork. Using a dough scraper or a sharp knife, divide the circle into eight equal wedges, being careful not to cut all the way through.

If you prefer to make nurses, monsters, or other shapes, roll out the dough between sheets of parchment paper, cut into biscuits with a suitably shaped pastry cutter or two, and transfer them to the prepared sheet pan, spacing them 1 inch (2.5 cm) apart. Gently press together any scraps, reroll them, cut out more biscuits, and add them to the pan. Chill and prick as for the petticoats.

Bake the shortbread until pale golden brown, 20–25 minutes. Transfer the pan to a wire rack. If you have made petticoat tails and the divisions have disappeared in the oven, use the dough scraper or knife to recut them while the shortbread is hot. Let the shortbread cool on the pan on the rack about 15 minutes, then transfer to the rack and let cool completely. Gently break apart the petticoats once they are cool.

1 cup plus 2 tablespoons (140 g) flour

2½ tablespoons rice flour

¼ cup (50 g) superfine sugar, plus 1 teaspoon for sprinkling

½ cup (115 g) cold butter, cut into small cubes

SISTER HILDA
Oh, gingerbread monsters. That's, er, novel.

SHELAGH
They're actually shortbread nurses. The girls wanted to make them nun-shaped, but I . . . I thought that might be seen as disrespectful.

SEASON 10:
EPISODE 1

GINGERBREAD NOT MEN

Gingerbread descends from Roman spiced breads, and early recipes use breadcrumbs, honey, and spice to make a thick mixture which was sometimes colored red. Later, as tastes and technology changed, several different types evolved, from the dark, sticky cakes of northern England, to the light, spongy Lebkuchen *of Germany. Many gingerbreads were stamped, shaped, or molded, and gingerbread figures became a popular fair food. By the nineteenth century, ginger was cheap, and treacle had replaced much of the sugar, making them even more affordable. The biscuits make ideal tree decorations—we see Reggie tucking into gingerbread Santas in the season 9 Christmas special. They keep for weeks in a sealed container.*

MAKES ALMOST THE ENTIRE RECURRING CAST AS OF SEASON 11 (15 ADULTS, 3 CHILDREN)

Line two sheet pans with parchment paper.

Sift together the flour, baking soda, ginger, and mixed spice into a large bowl. In a small saucepan, combine the butter, sugar, and golden syrup over low heat, and heat just until the butter melts. Do not allow to boil. Pour the butter mixture into the flour mixture, add the water, and mix well with a wooden spoon.

Shape the dough into a smooth, slightly greasy ball, pop it into a bowl, cover with a kitchen towel, and let stand for 1 hour to cool down. If you are not ready to bake yet, you can refrigerate it for a few hours or even up to overnight.

On a lightly floured work surface, roll out the dough about ¼ inch (6 mm) thick. Using biscuit or cookie cutters in the desired figure shapes, cut out as many figures as possible and transfer them to the prepared pans, spacing them about 1 inch (2.5 cm) apart. Gather up the scraps, press them together, reroll, and cut out more figures, adding them to the pans. Chill the figures for 30–45 minutes. About 15 minutes before baking, preheat the oven to 325°F (165°C).

Bake the figures until they are lightly browned and cooked through but still yield a little to the touch, 20–25 minutes. Transfer them—working carefully, as they will still be flexible—to wire racks and let cool completely.

When the figures are cool, mix up the royal icing according to the package instructions and divide it into as many bowls as colors you plan to use, then color the batches as desired. Spoon the icings into piping bags fitted with plain tips (or into small plastic bags with a corner cut off) and pipe the icings onto the figures to form capes, cardigans, hats, gowns, wimples, and—if you decide an occasional man is permissible after all—ties and jackets. Let set before serving.

1⅔ cups (200 g) flour, plus more for the work surface

½ teaspoon baking soda

1½ teaspoons ground ginger

½ teaspoon mixed spice

6 tablespoons (90 g) butter

¼ cup (50 g) sugar

2 tablespoons golden syrup

1 tablespoon water

TO DECORATE

¾–1 cup (150–200 g) royal icing mix

Powdered food coloring in colors of choice

TRIXIE
Is anything special happening on Guy Fawkes night?

SISTER JULIENNE
Sister Winifred has baked some gingerbread!

SISTER WINIFRED
It's not in the shape of a man or anything.

SEASON 6: EPISODE 7

MELTING MOMENTS

Even the name of these little shortbread-style biscuits screams postwar Britain. The Oxford English Dictionary *dates their first appearance in print to 1947, in a book written by the iconic Scottish cookery writer and scholar Florence Marian McNeill. She described them as "delicious little afternoon tea cakes." By 1957, they had moved south of the border, and a recipe was included in the BE-RO pamphlet. BE-RO was a flour manufacturer and had published a recipe booklet to publicize its products since 1923. It was free on demand and updated every few years. (However, the little girl on the 1950s editions was the same one who was in the 1930s pictures, with just slightly updated clothing. She looks a lot like a young Sister Frances.) It became a household staple, especially for those on tight budgets, and a lot of older people still regularly cook from it today. Even for the grandchildren of the* Call the Midwife *generation, it's still relevant, and still available, now in its forty-first iteration.*

MAKES 30–35 BISCUITS

Preheat the oven to 350°F (180°C). Line two sheet pans with parchment paper and butter the parchment, or line the pans with silicone baking mats.

In a bowl, using an electric mixer on medium-high speed or a wooden spoon, beat together the butter, lard, sugar, and salt until light in color and fluffy. Add the egg and vanilla, and beat until incorporated. Sift together the flour and baking powder into the butter-sugar mixture and then stir in gently just until fully incorporated. Shape the mixture into a loose ball.

Spread the oats on a plate. With slightly wet hands, divide the mixture into 30–35 portions and shape each portion into a ball. Roll each ball in the oats to coat on all sides and place on the prepared pans. Press down lightly on each ball to form a thick disk. Make sure they are well spaced, as they will spread during baking. About 2 inches (5 cm) should be ample enough.

Bake the biscuits until golden brown, 20–25 minutes. (One pan may be done first, so keep an eye on both of them.) Transfer the biscuits to wire racks and decorate each one with a small piece of glacé cherry, then let cool completely.

These are best eaten on the day they are made. Nobody seems to have an issue eating them fast, so storage is rarely a problem.

1960s SPIN *In the 1950s and 1960s, the coating was almost always rolled oats, though the BE-RO recipe suggested shredded dried coconut as an alternative. By the early 1970s, crushed cornflakes were creeping in, which is an ideal way to use up leftovers from the krackolates on page 62. Twenty years later, there were murmurs, eagerly fueled by Kellogg's, that Crunchy Nut Cornflakes could be used, but that's just too decadent for this book.*

5 tablespoons (70 g) unsalted butter, at room temperature, plus more for the pans if using parchment paper

3 tablespoons lard, at room temperature

⅓ cup plus 1½ tablespoons (85 g) superfine sugar

Pinch of salt

½ egg, lightly beaten (about 1½ tablespoons)

1 teaspoon pure vanilla extract

1 cup plus 2 tablespoons (140 g) flour

½ teaspoon baking powder

½ cup (50 g) old-fashioned rolled oats or (20 g) roughly crushed cornflakes

6–8 glacé cherries, cut into 30–35 small pieces, for decorating

PEPPERMINT STICKS

This recipe couldn't originate from any other decade than the 1960s. There are many similar recipes, but this is based on one by Margaret Bates, whose 1964 book, Talking About Cakes: with a Scottish and Irish Accent, *is gloriously silly and very good. Cornflakes are a staple breakfast in* Call the Midwife, *especially in the early seasons where the distinctive packaging appears in many a domestic morning scene. This is a way to use them in a rather more interesting fashion. Bates states that these peppermint-flavor sweets are "good with a cup of coffee." Whether you opt for the ubiquitous Poplar fix of a cup of Nescafé (instant coffee) or the more heady heights of a percolator or stove-top pot is entirely up to you.*

MAKES 24–30 STICKS

To make the bake, preheat the oven to 350°F (180°C). Line the bottom and sides of 13×9-inch (33×23-cm) baking pan with parchment paper.

In a bowl, combine the flour, coconut, superfine sugar, cocoa powder, and baking powder and stir to mix. Add the butter and peppermint extract and mix well. Add the cornflakes and stir just until evenly incorporated. Transfer the mixture to the prepared pan, pressing it onto the bottom to create an even layer just under ¼ inch (6 mm) thick.

Bake until set to the touch, about 20 minutes. Let cool in the pan on a wire rack to room temperature, then invert onto the rack, lift of the pan, and peel off the parchment.

To make the buttercream, in a bowl, whisk together the butter, cream cheese, confectioners' sugar, and peppermint extract until the mixture is light and spreadable. Set the cooled bake on a plate and, using a palette knife or an offset spatula, spread the buttercream on top. It doesn't have to be smooth, but it should be as even as possible.

To make the chocolate drizzle, melt the chocolate in a small heatproof bowl set over (not touching) simmering water in a small saucepan (or use a microwave) and let cool. In another small bowl, beat the butter with a wooden spoon until smooth and creamy, then beat the chocolate into the butter. The mixture will be quite runny. Pour this mixture into a piping bag fitted with a ⅛-inch (3-mm) plain tip (or use a plastic bag with the corner snipped off). Drizzle the mixture over the buttercream. The original recipe cheerfully suggests you make the pattern "random," but it is up to you.

Allow the buttercream and drizzle to firm up in the fridge for 30 minutes before cutting the sheet into 24–30 narrow sticks for serving.

FOR THE CAKE

1 cup (125 g) flour

1¼ cups (125 g) unsweetened shredded dried coconut

½ cup (100 g) superfine sugar

2 tablespoons unsweetened cocoa powder

1 teaspoon baking powder

¾ cup (170 g) butter, melted and cooled

½ teaspoon pure peppermint extract

1 cup (30 g) cornflakes, lightly crushed

FOR THE BUTTERCREAM

3 tablespoons butter, at room temperature

3 tablespoons cream cheese, at room temperature

1 cup (115 g) confectioners' sugar

1½ teaspoons pure peppermint extract

FOR THE CHOCOLATE DRIZZLE

1 oz (30 g) dark chocolate

Scant 1 tablespoon unsalted butter, at room temperature

BANANA OAT BISCUITS

A combination of bananas and porridge oats, these unassuming little biscuits are more like an American cookie than the crunchy British norm. Porridge is a standard breakfast food in Call the Midwife, *eaten by the Turners and at Nonnatus House, and is used as a comforting food for both breakfast and other meals in times of need. At the time, bananas were widely touted as a superfood, full of goodness and energy and loved by all. One contemporary advertisement proudly suggested the reader "unzip a banana . . . the foodiest fruit of all." These biscuits are very easy to make and keep well. They are an ideal teatime pick-me-up but would also be suitably fortifying for nurses on a busy district round.*

MAKES 12 BISCUITS

Preheat the oven to 400°F (200°C). Line a sheet pan with parchment paper or a silicone baking mat.

Sift the flour into a large bowl. Add the sugar, salt, baking soda, cinnamon, and nutmeg, and stir to mix. Scatter the butter over the flour mixture and, using a pastry blender or your fingertips, work it into the flour mixture just until the mixture is crumbly. Add the bananas, egg, oats, and oatmeal, and mix well with a wooden spoon. Stir in the nuts until evenly distributed.

Using two spoons, dollop the mixture onto the prepared sheet pan, forming 12 equal-size dollops and spacing them about 2 inches (5cm) apart. Bake the biscuits until the edges are browned but the centers remain soft to the touch, 15–20 minutes. Transfer to a wire rack and let cool completely before serving.

⅔ cup (85 g) flour

⅓ cup (85 g) sugar

½ teaspoon salt

¼ teaspoon baking soda

½ teaspoon ground cinnamon

Generous pinch of ground nutmeg

6 tablespoons (90 g) cold butter, cut into small cubes

3 ripe bananas, peeled and mashed (about 1¼ cups)

1 egg, lightly beaten

1 cup (100 g) old-fashioned rolled oats

½ cup (115 g) steel-cut oats

⅓ cup (35 g) chopped walnuts

SISTER MONICA JOAN

Put down the bananas. They are superfluous to the situation.

SEASON 4: EPISODE 1

EATING WITH THE NUNS

Mealtimes and their makeup were very class dependent in the 1950s and 1960s. For the majority of the population, the main meal of the day—usually called dinner—was served around midday or one o'clock and comprised hot food. Other meals fit around this focal point. Around 60 percent of workingmen went home for their midday meal, while others ate in canteens, restaurants, or cafés, or took sandwiches.

The people at Nonnatus House come from a mixture of backgrounds. Those who, like Sister Julienne or Sister Monica Joan, Chummy or Patsy, are from upper-class backgrounds would have grown up having dinner in the evening, with lunch a lighter meal in the middle of the day. However, the practicalities of life as working women in the East End mean that the pattern of eating at the nunnery follows that of the people they work with in the outside world.

The real Jenny Lee (writing under her married name, Jennifer Worth) wrote about the food she experienced at the convent that she fictionalized as Nonnatus House. Breakfast was "a pot of tea, boiled eggs, toast, home-made gooseberry jam, cornflakes, home-made yoghurt and scones." This was fuel for morning rounds, or a meal taken before collapsing into bed for those on the night shift. Dinner followed, made by Mrs. B, the "Queen of the Kitchen," and "an expert in steak and kidney pies, thick stews, savoury mince, toad-in-the-hole, treacle puddings, jam roly-poly, macaroni puddings and so on, as well as baking the best bread and cakes you could find anywhere." If you want to stage a Nonnatus House dinner, head for the recipes listed under Dinner Dishes and follow with something from Sweets.

The hot dinner at lunchtime was vital. The midwives cycled up to twenty miles (thirty-two km) a day, with morning visits followed by busy afternoon clinics. While habitual snacking was rare, surveys showed that around half the population habitually had elevenses (tea and a biscuit around 11:00 a.m.), and most also had some form of tea in the afternoon. For the leisured class, this was sometimes elevated to afternoon tea, a late-Victorian custom complete with sandwiches and cakes. We see Chummy and her mother in fashionable tearooms, as well as Trixie when she's dipping her toe into the dating waters. But for the majority, it was a mug or cup of tea and a biscuit around four or five o'clock.

Later still came the evening meal, usually around six or six thirty. It's a cold collation, though the Turners, who are more upwardly mobile as well as more modern, choose this point to have their hot dinner. Their meals

LUCILLE
It smells delicious. Thank you, Phyllis.

MISS HIGGINS
I might have a sandwich instead.

SISTER MONICA JOAN
Cold food is served at tea-time.

SEASON 11: EPISODE 2

offer us a glimpse into the fashionable foods of the time. Dishes such as coq au vin, *pommes duchesse*, and chicken à la King and the occasional glass of wine appear when Shelagh pushes the boat out. You'll find a selection of these recipes and some side dishes toward the end of Dinner Dishes. At Nonnatus House, the meal is more of a high tea. We see salads and sandwiches, tarts and quiches, along with a gala pie (pork with egg) that would have been bought from a local butcher rather than made in-house. These are followed by cake and washed down with yet more tea. Have a look at Cold Collations and then finish with a selection from Large Cakes if you want to put on a Nonnatus House high tea.

Only the upper classes, which include Matthew Aylward, dined at eight. Early teas could leave a gap, and around three-quarters of the population admitted to having a light supper to follow. In most cases, this was a simple snack of bread and cheese, or yet more biscuits. At Nonnatus House, anyone who gets peckish has the run of the larder, which is stocked with cakes, biscuits, preserves, and bread. Much was made by locals, donated by them to the nunnery, or bought via endless church bazaars and other such community events.

The residents of Nonnatus House eat very well. The food is plain but plentiful. To stage your own meal, you have lots of choices. Just remember to take joy in what you are eating—and don't forget the teapot.

DINNER DISHES

DELIA

*Do you suppose we'll go to hell? Sitting
eating our supper in the house of God?*

PATSY

Well, it's less of a crime than eating in the street.

SEASON 4: EPISODE 2

CHICKEN AND MUSHROOM PIE

Pies are a staple in Call the Midwife, *whether it's the traditional East End eel pie and mash or the pricier but popular steak (or steak and kidney) pie. Most of the pies we see on-screen are purchased from a pie shop—we see behind the scenes of one in season 2—and are either eaten in the shop or taken home to be reheated. Pies are time-consuming to make at home and require outlay on fuel for long cooking, and both time and money are in short supply for many of the families we see in the series. However, there are exceptions. In season 3, Chummy, bored and determined to improve her domestic skills, cooks chicken and mushroom pies for Nonnatus House. They aren't the greatest success, and when she eventually turns up with her pram full of food, it's newspaper-wrapped fish-and-chips that she dishes out—another takeout favorite and definitely not one to attempt at home.*

SERVES 4 AS A MAIN COURSE

In a large frying pan, melt 4 tablespoons (60 g) of the butter over medium heat. When the butter foams, add the chicken and fry, turning as needed and sprinkling on the flour about halfway through, until browned on all sides, about 10 minutes. Using a slotted spoon, transfer the chicken to a bowl and set aside.

Add the mushrooms and the remaining 2 tablespoons butter to the butter and chicken fat remaining in the pan and fry the mushrooms over medium heat, stirring occasionally, until they yield their water, about 10 minutes. Add the parsley and tarragon, mix well, and then add the mushrooms to the bowl holding the chicken.

Return the pan to high heat, add the wine, and deglaze the pan, scraping the bottom to dislodge all the sticky bits. Pour in the stock and bring to a boil. Remove from the heat and add to the chicken and mushrooms along with the mustard and cream. Season with salt and pepper, and mix well. Let cool until tepid, then cover and chill well (a warm filling will ruin the pastry). You can prepare the filling up to a day in advance.

When ready to bake, preheat the oven to 400°F (200°C). Butter the bottom and sides of 2 rectangular rimmed pie dishes, each 7×5½ inches (18×14 cm).

6 tablespoons (90 g) unsalted butter, plus more for the pie dishes

1 lb (450 g) boneless, skinless chicken thighs, cut into ¾-inch (2-cm) chunks

1 tablespoon flour, plus more for the work surface

¼ lb (115 g) white mushrooms, brushed clean and sliced

1 tablespoon chopped fresh flat-leaf parsley

2 teaspoons chopped fresh tarragon, or ½ teaspoon dried tarragon

6 tablespoons (90 ml) white wine

¾ cup (180 ml) chicken stock

1 tablespoon Dijon mustard

2 tablespoons heavy cream

Salt and pepper

1 lb (450 g) all-butter puff pastry, thawed according to package directions if frozen

Recipe continues on the following page

Continued from the previous page

Divide the pastry in half, and then divide each half into two pieces, one twice as large as the other. On a lightly floured work surface, roll out the larger piece of each half into a rectangle large enough to line each prepared dish, including a little overhang. Ease the pastry into the dishes, pressing it gently into the corners and up the sides. Divide the chilled chicken mixture between the lined dishes. Roll out the smaller pastry pieces into rectangles to form a lid for each dish. Dampen the edges of the bottom pastry on both pies with water, then top each pie with its lid, crimping the edges together well to seal and trimming away any excess pastry. Cut a small slash in the center of each pie to allow steam to escape. Or if you like, use a pie bird—aka pie funnel, pie chimney, or pie whistle—to vent the steam, as pictured on page 85. Put the bird in the center of the pastry-lined dish, add the filling around it, and top with the pastry lid, cutting a hole in the center for the head of the bird to pass through.

Bake the pies until the pastry is golden and puffed and the filling is heated through, 30–35 minutes. Remove from the oven, let cool for a few minutes, and then cut each pie in half and use a wide spatula to serve.

CHUMMY
Now I then fold the pastry over—like so! And then repeat the action four times, whilst the pie filling simmers on a low light!

SEASON 3: EPISODE 1

POTATO AND ONION PIE

There's a lot of potato peeling in Call the Midwife. *It is particularly prevalent in the season 9 Christmas special, when the nurses huddle around the fire clad in everything they possess in an attempt to stave off the rain and chill in the Outer Hebrides. Potato preparation is an easy kitchen activity to make people look like they are bustling, but it also reflects the plain nature of food for the majority of people in the 1950s and 1960s. Potatoes were everywhere: mashed, boiled, baked, chipped (or french fries, as they are known in the States), and very occasionally roasted. This recipe has eighteenth century origins, from the time when potatoes first became popular as a food for the masses, but it was a staple of the* Call the Midwife *era, too. Unsurprisingly, it was popular as a vegetarian dish and was included on the menu at the highly fashionable Cranks restaurant, which was widely credited with changing perceptions of vegetarian cuisine in the 1960s and 1970s. Its version, which was an open pie, was called homity pie, and the recipe first appeared under that name in the 1982 Cranks recipe book. We see Sister Hilda prepare one in season 11. If you want to pep this pie up a little, add a few handfuls of sharp cheese, such as Cheddar, or some finely diced bacon.*

SERVES 6–8 AS A MAIN COURSE

To make the pastry, put the flour into a bowl and scatter the butter over the top. Using a pastry blender, cut the butter into the flour until butter is in pieces the size of small peas. Drizzle the egg and 1 tablespoon of the water evenly over the flour mixture and, using as few strokes as possible, stir and toss with a fork, adding just enough additional water, a little at a time, as needed for the dough to come together in a shaggy mass. Do not overwork. (This is easiest done in a food processor, first pulsing the butter into the flour and then pulsing in the egg and water.) Gently knead the dough in the bowl just enough to bring it together in a thick disk, then cover the bowl with a plate and refrigerate for 30 minutes.

Preheat the oven to 425°F (220°C). Butter a rimmed rectangular pie dish about 10×6 inches (25×15cm).

To make the filling, arrange a layer of potato slices in the prepared dish, dot with some of the butter, and season generously with pepper (you should not need salt if your butter is salted). Top with a layer of onion, dot with butter, and season generously with pepper. Repeat the layers until all the potato slices and onion are used, ending with butter and pepper. Evenly pour the stock over the top.

On a lightly floured work surface, roll out the pastry into a rectangle 1/4 inch (6 mm) thick. Trim the rectangle to fit the top of the dish with a little overhang. Carefully top the dish with the pastry, crimping the edges to the rim. Cut a small slash in the center of the pie to allow steam to escape. Or better still, use a pie bird (pastry funnel), standing it in the filling and cutting a small hole in the pastry so the bird pokes out the top. Brush the pastry with the glaze.

Bake the pie until the top is golden brown, about 45 minutes. Let cool for a few minutes, then cut into squares and scoop out with a spoon to serve.

FOR THE PASTRY

1 3/4 cups plus 1 tablespoon (225 g) flour, plus more for the work surface

1/2 cup (115 g) cold butter, cut into small cubes, plus more for the pie dish

1 egg, lightly beaten

2–3 tablespoons ice-cold water

FOR THE FILLING

1 lb (450 g) waxy potatoes, peeled and sliced 1/8 inch (3 mm) thick

1/2 cup (115 g) butter

White or black pepper

1 yellow onion, minced

1 cup (240 ml) chicken or vegetable stock

1 egg, beaten with a generous pinch of salt and 1 teaspoon water, for glazing

FISH PIE

The sea is omnipresent in Call the Midwife. *Many of the men we meet are employed at the West India Docks, then the main hub for imports into London, and the noise and smell of the working dockyard forms a permanent backdrop to life in Poplar. From time to time, we're reminded more directly of the importance of the area. Season 6 is particularly focused on the docks, from the episode 2 explosion when we first meet Valerie Dyer to the workers' strike for more humane conditions. The sea is also a critical source of food. We regularly see signs advertising dabs and sprats (small fish usually sold whole in oil or smoked). And we get a close look at a fish stall in season 5, episode 6, when the mother and daughter running it seek to hide an illegitimate conception with disastrous consequences. Typical of workers' food, this pie is made of fish offcuts that could be cheaply bought at the end of the day and potato mocked up to resemble a pastry crust. Today, Billingsgate fish market is located in Poplar, where it moved in 1982 after hundreds of years in the center of London.*

SERVES 4–6 AS A MAIN COURSE

To make the mash, in a saucepan, combine the potatoes with salted water to cover and bring to a boil over high heat. Reduce the heat to a simmer, and simmer until the potatoes are tender, 10–20 minutes, depending on the size of the chunks. Drain well, return to the pan, and mash with a handheld masher, adding the butter piece by piece as you go. Set aside.

While the potatoes are cooking, preheat the oven to 350°F (180°C). Butter an 8-inch (20-cm) round ceramic pie dish.

To make the filling, first make a brown béchamel sauce. Pour the milk into a small saucepan and heat over medium heat just until hot, then remove from the heat. While the milk is heating, in a medium saucepan, melt the butter over medium-low heat. Sprinkle in the flour, then stir the butter and flour constantly with a wooden spoon until the butter browns slightly (becoming beurre noisette) and forms a light brown paste with the flour, about 4 minutes. Add the hot milk, 2–3 tablespoons at a time, whisking well after each addition. Then continue to stir over medium heat until you have a fairly thick, smooth, pale-brown sauce. Stir in the cream and season with the nutmeg and with salt and pepper to taste.

Remove the sauce from the heat and stir in the fish, shrimp, and parsley, making sure all the seafood is coated with the sauce. Transfer the mixture to the prepared dish. Top with the mash, smoothing it evenly over the surface to the edge of the dish. Then use a fork to make crimped patterns around the edge to resemble crimped pastry. You can also put a few holes in the center for extra authenticity. Brush the top with the egg wash.

FOR THE MASH

2 lb (900 g) potatoes (about 2 large baking potatoes), peeled and roughly chopped

½ cup (115 g) butter, plus more for the pie dish

FOR THE FILLING

½ cup (120 ml) milk

1 tablespoon butter

1 tablespoon flour

1 cup (240 ml) heavy cream

Pinch of ground nutmeg

Salt and pepper

1½ lb (600 g) skinless fish fillets (see Recipe Note), cut into pieces roughly ¾ inch (2 cm) square

3½ oz (100 g) shrimp, peeled and deveined

2 tablespoons chopped fresh flat-leaf parsley

1 egg, beaten with a pinch of salt, for egg wash

Bake the pie until the top is golden brown and a metal skewer inserted into the center for a few seconds comes out piping hot to the touch, 30–35 minutes. Serve right away.

RECIPE NOTE You can use any fish for this pie, though it is best with a mixture of white fish, such as cod and haddock, and oily fish, including salmon and trout. If you can't get raw shrimp, use cooked ones or leave them out. You can also mix in crabmeat or lobster meat or other shellfish. The pie needs only a vegetable side to make it a complete meal. Or you can make it an all-in-one bake by adding 2 cups (400 g) chopped, blanched, and well-drained spinach or 2 cups (280 g) peas (tinned or frozen is fine) to the sauce when you mix in the fish. If you prefer your mash with the skin on, simply scrub the potatoes rather than peel them.

TRIXIE
My godmother insisted we spent a week shopping in Paris, so she could send me back to London prepared for every style eventuality.

LUCILLE
Does she know which bit of London you live in?

TRIXIE
She knows that a woman is defined by her potential and not her circumstances, and that one exquisite black shift dress from a top couturier can take you anywhere, even out for dinner with an Italian count.

LUCILLE
An Italian count? I bet he never bought you the last piece of haddock in the chip shop!

SEASON 8:
CHRISTMAS

TOAD IN THE HOLE

Toad in the hole appears in season 6, episode 3, as part of the process of cultural assimilation around the supper table. Thoroughly Liverpudlian Lucy Chen makes it for her equally thoroughly Chinese mother-in-law, who is first shocked and then accepting, reflecting the family's own story arc in the episode, which also involves carbon monoxide poisoning and a near death thanks to Sister Ursula's efficiency drive. Toad is effectively a savory batter pudding. When it first became popular in the late eighteenth century, the filling could be anything from a small roast to brains wrapped in bacon, but it was most commonly used to eke out leftover cooked meat or cheap cuts of fresh meat. By the 1950s, it generally involved sausages, and today most people have no idea that a toad can contain almost anything you fancy. In the show, it's served with carrots, but it works well with any vegetable side. To be truly 1950s, the vegetables should be tinned, but that is entirely up to you.

SERVES 4 AS A MAIN COURSE

Start with the batter. Sift the flour into a large bowl. Add the salt, eggs, and milk, and whisk until the mixture is very homogenous and slightly frothy, about 15 minutes. This is best done in a stand mixer fitted with the paddle attachment or with a handheld mixer on medium speed. Let rest for 15–20 minutes.

Meanwhile, put a 10–12-inch (25–30-cm) cast-iron frying pan into the oven and preheat the oven to 425°F (220°C).

In a large saucepan, combine the sausages with just enough water to cover and bring to a boil over medium-high heat. Adjust the heat to a gentle simmer and poach the sausages for 5–10 minutes, then drain. (You can omit this step, but it does make the sausages lovely and moist and means you don't need to overcook your batter to ensure the sausages are fully cooked.)

When the oven comes to temperature, put the lard into the hot pan and return it to the oven to heat for a couple of minutes. Then add the poached sausages to the pan and bake just until they start to sizzle and brown, 5–10 minutes.

Remove the pan from the oven and, using a heat-resistant brush, coat the sides of the pan with the melted fat. Add the batter to the pan, drizzling it into the hot fat and over the sausages. Return the pan to the oven and bake until the pudding is puffed up and dark brown (but not burnt) and the tops of the sausages are visibly well cooked, 35–40 minutes. The interior of the pudding should still be moist and pleasingly stodgy.

Serve immediately, accompanied with a large jug of hot gravy. The gravy should be sufficiently thick that the traditional British call of "one lump or two" makes total sense.

1¼ cups (150 g) flour

1 teaspoon salt

2 eggs

1 cup plus 2½ tablespoons (275 ml) milk

8 plain pork sausages

2 tablespoons lard or meat drippings

2 cups (480 ml) gravy (made from a mix is fine)

LUCY
It's called toad-in-the-hole.

OILEN
Toad?

LUCY
(laughs) Well, not really. It's a sausage.

SEASON 6: EPISODE 3

MULLIGATAWNY SOUP

Mulligatawny soup was one of the culinary legacies of empire. In Call the Midwife, *we watch as the ethnic makeup of Poplar changes, including the arrival and integration of many families of Indian, Bangladeshi, and Pakistani descent. They would barely have recognized what passed for Indian-inspired food in the homes of the white population around them. Mulligatawny was described by one contemporary writer, aiming, admittedly, at a slightly different market from the people of Poplar: "This Anglo-Indian concoction is a modified Madras curry, served as a soup. It is a wonderful thing to carry in a vacuum bottle on a hunting, or fishing, trip in zero weather." It was originally made as both a thick soup stuffed with meat (usually mutton) and vegetables and a thinner consommé. However, as most people bought it in tins and got used to that version, eventually it settled into being just plain old mulligatawny, a mildly spiced and warming household favorite. And yes, it would be ideal in a Thermos, shared between old friends on a park bench or stuffed into a bike basket in case of need during a long delivery.*

SERVES 2 AS A LIGHT SUPPER OR 4 AS A STARTER

In a saucepan, melt the butter over low heat. Add the onion and cook gently, stirring occasionally, until it starts to become translucent, 10–15 minutes. Add the carrot, raise the heat to medium, and cook, stirring occasionally, until the carrot softens and starts to brown, about 10 minutes. Add the apple and then sprinkle in the curry powder, cayenne (if using), flour, and salt. Stir well and cook, stirring often, for a few minutes more.

Now add the thyme (it is up to you whether you strip off the leaves and add them or add the whole sprigs), parsley, and bay leaves, and pour in the stock. Bring to a boil over medium-high heat, stirring constantly, then reduce the heat to a low simmer. Cover and cook for 30 minutes, stirring occasionally to prevent sticking.

Remove the pan from the heat, and remove and discard the whole herbs. Use an immersion blender to purée the soup in the pan, or let cool for a few minutes, transfer the soup to a stand blender, purée until smooth, and then return the soup to the pan.

Return the pan to medium-low heat, add the lemon juice, taste, and adjust the seasoning with salt if needed. Stir in the cream and finally the rice, mixing well. Heat until piping hot, then serve.

2 tablespoons butter

1 small yellow onion, diced

1 carrot, peeled and diced

1 eating apple, peeled, cored, and diced

1 tablespoon curry powder

Pinch of cayenne pepper (optional)

1½ tablespoons flour

1 teaspoon salt

2 fresh thyme sprigs

1 tablespoon chopped fresh flat-leaf parsley

2 bay leaves

5 cups (1.2 l) lamb or beef stock, heated

Juice of ½ lemon

2 tablespoons heavy cream

½ cup (100 g) cooked rice

TOMATO SOUP

By the 1950s, modern marketing techniques were starting to come to the fore. One such was the public poll, designed to reflect the nation's tastes but usually commissioned with an ulterior motive in mind. Between 1947 and 1973, Gallup polled the British on their ideal meal, money no object. It turned out people were fonder of good soup than grilled grouse, and they really liked sherry, trifle, and roasted potatoes. Tomato soup topped the polls consistently. Most people's experience of it would have been in tins, but it was also easy to make. Tomatoes—or at least a reference to them—appear in the very first episode of Call the Midwife, *when a new father asks for the afterbirth to fuel his allotment. It won't be the first time.*

SERVES 4–6 AS A STARTER

In a large saucepan, melt the butter over medium heat. Add the onion, celery, carrot, garlic, and bacon (if using) and cook, stirring occasionally, until the vegetables are softened, 15–20 minutes. Set aside off the heat.

In a small saucepan, bring the stock just to a simmer, then remove from the heat. While the stock is heating, core and cut up the tomatoes: in quarters if using standard-size tomatoes, in eighths if using beefsteak tomatoes, and in half if using cherry tomatoes (unknown in the 1960s). Add the tomatoes to the pan holding the onion mixture along with the tomato paste and sugar. Pour in the hot stock and pop in the bouquet garni.

Bring to a boil over medium-high heat, stirring to prevent scorching, then reduce the heat to a gentle simmer, and simmer, stirring occasionally, for 30 minutes. The tomatoes will be broken down and soft.

Remove from the heat, and remove and discard the bouquet garni. Use an immersion blender to purée the soup in the pan, or let cool for a few minutes, transfer the soup to a stand blender, purée until smooth, and then return the soup to the pan.

Return the pan to medium-low heat and season the soup with salt and pepper. If you like, stir in the cream, which makes this into cream of tomato soup. Heat until piping hot, then ladle into bowls and top with croutons, if desired (though you wouldn't have seen them in Poplar in the 1950s). Serve at once.

3 tablespoons butter

1 small yellow onion, diced

1 celery rib, diced

1 carrot, peeled and diced

2 cloves garlic, minced

1 slice bacon, chopped (optional)

4¼ cups (1 l) chicken or vegetable stock

2½ lb (1.1 kg) ripe tomatoes

2 teaspoons tomato paste (UK purée)

Pinch of sugar

Bouquet garni of 2 fresh thyme sprigs, 2 bay leaves, and 1 fresh rosemary sprig, tied together with kitchen string

Salt and pepper

¼ cup (60 ml) heavy cream (optional)

Croutons, for serving (optional)

OVERSEAS INFLUENCES

Britain has always been a multicultural nation. Its cuisine is a mishmash of influences from Europe and beyond. Whether it's the adoption of Jewish fried fish and South American potatoes fried in a French (or possibly Belgian) manner as a national dish—fish and chips—or the daily downing of a Chinese drink grown largely in India and Africa—tea—there are very few apparently British dishes that haven't been influenced by global foodways. However, beyond the generalities of historical British cuisine, *Call the Midwife* is very good at highlighting specific ways in which the world of food was changing in line with the population of Britain in the 1950s and 1960s.

The changing makeup of Poplar throughout the seasons of *Call the Midwife* reflects real changes in Britain itself. Prewar, Britain had already seen mass immigration, particularly from Germany in the late nineteenth century and Jewish refugees from Europe in the twentieth century. We see the influence of Jewish culture on foods in several episodes, watching as families celebrate with challah and strudel and buy specialist provisions from Jewish delis in the East End. There were large numbers of Italians as well, who dominated the ice cream trade.

But now new communities sought better lives in Britain, either of their own volition, or, as with the Caribbean community, with the active encouragement of the British government desperate for workers in the state-owned industries, the National Rail, the Royal Mail, and the National Health Service in particular.

In *Call the Midwife*, we meet several Chinese families who have taken advantage of the link between Hong Kong and Britain. Chinese restaurants were one of the first types of overtly foreign cuisine to spread to a specifically British audience outside London (previous Chinese restaurants were opened primarily to serve the Chinese community). We witness culinary assimilation in action as the Chen family eat a mixture of traditional Chinese food—fish soup—and British fare—toad in the hole. Meanwhile, in 1965, 31 percent of respondents to a survey on eating out reported they had been to a Chinese restaurant.

India was the next big influence. The messy withdrawal of Britain from India in the 1940s led to civil war. Many Indian families immigrated to Britain. Restaurants were an obvious way to make a living, taking advantage of both the existing

> **LUCILLE**
> *I had no idea there's a café serving Caribbean food.*
>
> **CYRIL**
> *I'm so pleased you like it. I heard about this place from Albert at the social club.*
>
> **LUCILLE**
> *It tastes like home. I've missed it so much.*
>
> SEASON 9: EPISODE 3

British familiarity with Indian food and the boom in eating out following the war. The British called everything vaguely Indian a curry and had long since taken the general idea to heart. Curries first appeared in printed British recipe books in the eighteenth century. The word *curry* has Tamil origins, but was—and is—used as a catchall for any spicy and stew-like dish. But the mainly Sylheti settlers were adaptable. The restaurant that Tom takes Barbara to in season 5 would have served quite different food to that which we see in the homes of the various Indian, Pakistani, or Bangladeshi mothers, and was very novel. The growth of curry houses was really a 1970s tale.

The final group we see close at hand in *Call the Midwife* is the Caribbean community. Caribbean food was far slower to spread through restaurants. When we see Lucille and Cyril eating in a Caribbean café in season 9, it's clear that this is a shop that also serves meals and is aimed squarely at Black émigrés, rather than the whites who surround them. When the residents at Nonnatus House sample jerk chicken, rice and peas, and dumplings as part of the meal they've arranged to make Lucille feel more welcome after she faces racism in season 7, they are very lucky indeed.

GRAPEFRUIT SURPRISE

One of the lovely things about Call the Midwife *is that because each season covers one year, we are always the same distance in time—55 years—from the events in Poplar as we were when the series started. While the sets (mainly) remain the same, small details mark the passing of time: Plastic bowls replace metal and ceramic, synthetic fibers replace wool and linen, and new foods are introduced or popularized. From Cynthia's avocado in season 1 (greeted with a decided lack of enthusiasm) to the summer squashes of season 10, we share with the characters the delight of the new and are reminded that numerous foods we take for granted now were still novelties for many just half a century ago. A citrus hybrid, grapefruits date to the late eighteenth century and were first grown commercially in California a century later. They remained an American choice, largely eaten for breakfast, until the 1930s, when the success of the American Olympians at the 1936 Olympics piqued wider interest. Their move to the dinner table came later. In the 1960s, grilled grapefruit was delightfully different. It's unfashionable now, but like so many dishes of the time, it might be ripe for a comeback.*

SERVES 2 AS A SIDE

Preheat the broiler.

Cut the grapefruit in half crosswise. If needed, cut a thin slice from the bottom of each half so the halves will stand upright. Using a grapefruit knife or paring knife, cut around the edge of each half to loosen the flesh from the rind. Then cut along both sides of each segment to loosen the segments from the membranes (this makes the segments easier and less messy to eat), being careful not to cut through the rind. Spread the top of each grapefruit half with half of the honey.

Place the grapefruit halves on a small sheet pan and slide under the broiler. Broil until the honey is bubbling but not burnt and the top has softened, 6–8 minutes.

Pop a glacé cherry onto the center of each grapefruit half and serve.

1 white or pink grapefruit

1 tablespoon honey or Demerara sugar

2 glacé cherries

1960s SPIN Woman's Realm *published a recipe for grapefruit surprise in February 1960. The magazine titled its version American Grapefruit and added ⅓ tablespoon sherry along with the sweetener to each half before cooking. Given Trixie's struggles with alcohol, it seems inappropriate here, but if it suits you, it is a tasty addition.*

TRIXIE
It's called a "grapefruit surprise" (said with a French accent). The surprise (now in an English accent), in my case, being that sugar burns remarkably quickly under the grill

SEASON 7:
EPISODE 2

SHRIMP COCKTAIL

Shrimp cocktail is one of those dishes that is frequently lampooned and yet still holds a place in many people's hearts. Cocktails of this sort (salad with shellfish and a mayonnaise-based sauce) came out of America in the late nineteenth century and became very popular between the wars, when they were often served in cocktail glasses—theoretically, if not actually, out of use due to Prohibition in the States. By the late 1960s, seafood cocktails were the height of dinner-party sophistication among the middle classes, forming part of the perfect meal according to one survey of 1973, though it has to be admitted they were often quite bad. This version is adapted from the 1961 centenary edition of Mrs. Beeton's Book of Household Management, *which had been in print continuously (albeit with many changes) for one hundred years and was relied upon by housewives across the country. Cooks such as Mrs. Turner would have used freshly cooked shell-on shrimp (UK prawns) from one of the many shellfish stalls in Poplar. Today, it's easy to buy ready-picked (peeled) shrimp. But do avoid the tiny, shriveled things that lurk in the freezer cabinets and, as with all fish and shellfish, look for an indication that they have been responsibly farmed.*

SERVES 4 AS A STARTER OR 2 AS A LIGHT MEAL

To make the cocktail sauce—also known as Marie Rose sauce—in a small bowl, stir together the mayonnaise, tomato paste, tarragon vinegar, and Tabasco sauce to taste. Cover and refrigerate until needed.

Shrimp cocktail is ideally presented in a clear-glass bowl. This recipe assumes you are using one large one, but you can also serve it in individual glasses. Whichever you are using, start with the lettuce. Mix it with the salt and then layer it in the bowl or glasses. It should come about halfway up the sides. Next, add the shrimp, which should just about cover the lettuce.

Now cover the shrimp with your sauce, forming a smooth layer, and sprinkle the sauce with a little paprika. Garnish the dish with the tail-on shrimp, positioning them leaping in a sprightly manner over the sides of the bowl or glass. (Or, if serving in glasses, you can instead stand the tail-on shrimp on top of the layer of shrimp, then spoon on the sauce and top with paprika.) Finish with the lemon, either sliced and attached to the rim, cocktail-style, or in wedges.

Refrigerate until needed, but it is best served as soon as it is made lest the lettuce start to brown and wilt. You can also add avocado, though this is decidedly outré for 1950s Poplar.

½ cup (120 ml) mayonnaise (homemade or good-quality store-bought)

1 tablespoon tomato paste (UK purée)

1 teaspoon tarragon vinegar

4–5 drops Tabasco sauce, or 1 teaspoon chile vinegar

½ small head iceberg lettuce, chopped (about 2 cups/115 g)

½ teaspoon salt

7 oz (200 g) cooked, peeled, and deveined shrimp, plus 6–8 peeled with tail intact, for garnish

Paprika, for sprinkling

1 lemon

COQ AU VIN

The postwar period was one in which many of the dishes we think of as age-old now first came to true prominence. Dishes such as beef Wellington, shrimp cocktail, and coq au vin had, in many cases, earlier roots, but they were either reinvented or properly popularized in this new era of plenty (for some, anyway). Coq au vin started out as a French peasant dish, a way to make use of a tough male chicken (rooster) by simmering it for hours in cheap wine and whatever vegetables were to hand. In the early twentieth century, as metropolitan food writers discovered the culinary traditions of the wider country, it suddenly sparked the imagination. By the 1950s, it was usually made with a female chicken (hen), then a very expensive meat, and had a whiff of both the excitingly foreign and the reassuringly traditional about it. Because of the expense, it was a middle-class dish, thus in Call the Midwife *we see it served at the Turners' house. French tradition uses whatever wine is native to the region, so you can easily trade out the red wine used here for white or even* vin jaune. *But the red does give the bird a glorious color. If you aren't keen on onions (for example, if you're Violet Buckle and you have Nurse Anderson's wedding dress hanging in your flat), simply increase the celery and carrot and leave the onions out. Serve this classic with green beans and rice or potatoes.*

SERVES 6 AS A MAIN COURSE

If you are using a whole chicken, skin it and cut it into serving pieces. In a large, heavy pot (a Le Creuset is ideal), heat the butter and bacon over medium-high heat until the butter foams. Add the chicken pieces and cook, turning as needed, until browned on all sides, 6–8 minutes. (Brown the chicken in batches if needed to avoid crowding, transferring each batch to a plate as it is ready, and return them all to the pot after all have been browned.)

Reduce the heat slightly, add the onions, and cook, stirring often, until they start to brown, 10–15 minutes. Add the celery, carrot, and garlic, and cook for 5 minutes longer. Now add the mushrooms and thyme, season with salt and pepper, and pour in the wine and stock.

Raise the heat to high, bring to a boil, and cook uncovered for 10 minutes. Reduce the heat to a simmer and cook, turning the chicken occasionally, until the chicken is tender and dark red and the sauce has reduced to about one-third, about 1 hour.

1 whole free-range chicken, about 4 lb (1.8 kg), or 6 good-size bone-in, skinless chicken thighs

½ cup (115 g) unsalted butter

¼ lb (115 g) bacon, chopped

2 yellow onions, diced

1 celery rib, diced

1 small carrot, peeled and diced

2 cloves garlic, diced

6 oz (170 g) white mushrooms, brushed clean and sliced

Leaves from 2 fresh thyme sprigs

Salt and pepper

1 bottle (750 ml) red wine (not too gutsy, look for Bordeaux style)

1 cup (240 ml) chicken stock

¼ cup (60 ml) brandy

1 tablespoon arrowroot, mixed with 1 tablespoon water

Recipe continues on the following page

Continued from the previous page

Using tongs and a slotted spoon, transfer all the solids to a warmed plate and keep warm. Raise the heat to high, add the brandy, bring to a boil, and boil for 2–3 minutes. Taste and adjust the seasoning if needed. Finally, add the arrowroot mixture, mixing well, and then stir until the sauce thickens and becomes chocolaty, 2–3 minutes. (You can use a different thickening agent, but arrowroot gives the sauce a beautiful gloss.) Reduce the heat to medium (boiling too long lessens the thickening properties of arrowroot), return the chicken and other solids to the pot, and stir to ensure everything is well coated with the sauce and piping hot, then serve.

1960s SPIN *Wine was more aspired to than necessarily drunk in the 1950s and 1960s. It had long been seen as the province of the wealthy, and with rising living standards, it started to become more mainstream, though for most it was confined to dinner parties and special occasions. Certain brands did become household names, selling to the middle classes who were unsure of what to buy and needed something safe. In the show, we see some of the most iconic of these labels: Mateus Rosé, a Portuguese big hitter that came in a basket, and Liebfraumilch, which was a German Riesling. Meanwhile, Timothy admits to having tried yet another German Riesling, Blue Nun, which was explicitly designed for export and marketed as a wine you could drink "right through the meal," thus taking the worry out of inadvertently making a social faux pas when trying to impress friends with the right choice of wine.*

SHELAGH
I'll get your supper. Magda did a coq au vin.

DR. TURNER
Ooh, delicious!

SHELAGH
If you like that kind of thing.

SEASON 7: EPISODE 2

CHICKEN À LA KING

With its vaguely French name and use of what was, in the 1950s, a very expensive core ingredient—the chicken—this is very much an aspirational middle-class dish. Shelagh serves it to the rest of the Turner family in episode 5 of season 6, along with molded potatoes and creamed spinach. It originated in the United States in the late nineteenth century and comes with a few possible origin tales, including that it was named for the proprietor of the Brighton Beach Hotel, in the New York City borough of Brooklyn, and invented for him by that season's chef, George Greenwald. However, it didn't appear in print until 1912, and the early recipes were a riff on fairly standard chicken dishes from the classic French repertoire. By the time Shelagh cooks it, in 1960, it was usually made with peppers and mushrooms. Accompany the dish with rice or pasta and a vegetable.

SERVES 2–4 AS A MAIN COURSE

If using a raw red pepper, preheat the oven to 400°F (200°C). Halve the pepper lengthwise, remove the seeds, and cut each half into four pieces. Place the pieces in a small baking dish and bake until soft, about 8 minutes. Transfer the pieces to a covered bowl and set aside for 10 minutes. You should then be able to peel off the skin very easily. Dice the skinned pieces. If using a jarred pimiento, dice the flesh.

In a saucepan, melt the butter over medium heat. Add the green pepper and mushrooms, and cook, stirring occasionally, until soft, about 10 minutes. Sprinkle the flour over the vegetables and then stir until well combined with the pan juices. Slowly add the stock, stirring continuously until a thick sauce forms.

Add the chicken pieces to the sauce, turning them to ensure they are well coated. Reduce the heat to a gentle simmer and cook, stirring often to prevent sticking, until the chicken is cooked, about 12 minutes. Stir in the red pepper pieces.

In a bowl, stir together the sour cream, egg yolks, and sherry, mixing well, then whisk in 2–3 tablespoons of the sauce from the pan. Pour over the chicken mixture and stir over medium heat until the sauce is thick and glossy, about 5 minutes. Do not allow to boil. Season with salt, pepper, and a squeeze of lemon.

Serve piping hot, dusted with the paprika and parsley.

1 red bell pepper or jarred large pimiento

2 tablespoons unsalted butter

1 green or yellow bell pepper (not red, as it will turn the sauce pink), seeded and finely minced

½ cup (60 g) sliced white button mushrooms

1 tablespoon flour

1 cup (240 ml) chicken stock

2 boneless, skinless chicken breasts, cut into ½-inch (12-mm) cubes

⅔ cup (150 g) sour cream

2 egg yolks

1 tablespoon sherry

Salt and pepper

½ lemon

¼ teaspoon paprika

Leaves from 1 small bunch fresh flat-leaf parsley, minced

COURGETTES IN CREAM

The British infatuation with marrows is a hard thing to explain but nevertheless persisted for a couple of centuries before the gradual realization that baby marrows—courgettes—were infinitely preferable. The name comes from the French and effectively means small squashes, what in the States would be zucchini. They first started appearing in specialist vegetable cookery books in the 1930s, but it was an uphill struggle to persuade the British to embrace them. One reason was the obsession with gardening shows, something we see a lot in Call the Midwife, *where prizes were awarded for size but rarely for flavor. One 1960s vegetarian book lamented that "the enormous harvest-festival type are fine specimens to look at but they . . . [tend] to be tough and tasteless, all the goodness having passed into the seeds." Another problem was the generally poor treatment of vegetables in the British culinary tradition, which largely consisted of boiling them to smithereens and adding (if you were lucky) butter or margarine. This recipe is how the Turners eat them (or rather, how Shelagh prepares them, as Patrick and Timothy are rather more interested in the meat cutlets).*

SERVES 2 AS A SIDE

Cut the courgettes in half lengthwise and then slice crosswise into half-moons about ¼ inch (6 mm) thick.

In a frying pan, melt the butter over medium heat until it foams. Add the courgettes and cook, stirring often, until slightly softened, 2–3 minutes. Add the water, cover the pan, and cook for 2–3 minutes longer. Uncover, reduce the heat to low, stir in the cream and parsley, and heat through. Season with salt and pepper, add the zest, and serve.

RECIPE NOTE Garlic was generally eschewed in the 1960s—perhaps a clove would be wiped around a bowl in a daring fashion, but it wasn't very common. However, a couple of minced cloves briefly browned before adding the courgettes enhances this dish.

2–3 courgettes (zucchini), about ¾ lb (340 g) total weight

2 tablespoons butter

2 tablespoons water

¼ cup (60 ml) heavy cream

2 teaspoons finely chopped fresh flat-leaf parsley

Salt and pepper

Finely grated zest of ½ lemon

CREAMED SPINACH

This dish is served up at the Turners' celebratory meal before the disastrous camping trip in season 5. Spinach was easy to grow and edible year-round, making it a mainstay of the allotment, but it also came in cans. It is a good source of iron as well as several other vitamins, and we see Nurse Crane suggest it in lieu of liver to a fellow vegetarian in season 9. Creamed spinach is a decidedly more interesting way to serve it than the usual 1950s fallback of overboiling. This recipe is a riff on one from Lily MacLeod's Cooking for the Wayward Diabetic, *a condition we hear quite a bit about in* Call the Midwife, *as insulin injections formed part of the district round, and the daily insulin delivery is a good excuse for characters from the surgery to interact with those from Nonnatus House.*

Freezers were rare in the United Kingdom until the 1970s, so although the Call the Midwife *characters wouldn't have used frozen spinach, it does work here. Try to get the whole-leaf stuff rather than the chopped blocks though, as they tend to disintegrate.*

SERVES 4 AS A SIDE

Rinse the spinach well, then put it into a colander in the sink. Bring a kettle of water to a boil and pour the boiling water over the spinach to blanch it. Drain and then squeeze as much excess water out as possible. Transfer the spinach to a cutting board and chop it roughly.

In a high-sided frying pan with a lid, melt the butter over medium heat until it foams. Reduce the heat to medium-low, add the onion, and cook, stirring occasionally, until translucent and soft, 3–5 minutes. Add the cream, raise the heat to medium or medium-high, bring to a boil, and boil until reduced by about one-third, 3–4 minutes. Season with salt and pepper.

Adjust the heat to medium if needed, add two-thirds of the cheese to the pan, and stir to melt. Then add the chopped spinach, stir to mix well, and cover the pan to heat the spinach through and cook it properly. After about 5 minutes, remove the lid, stir it, and remove from the heat.

To finish the dish, preheat the broiler or have a kitchen torch on hand. Transfer the spinach to a broiler-proof serving bowl and smooth the top, or if the frying pan is broiler-proof and you feel it is suitable as a serving vessel, leave the spinach in the pan. Top evenly with the remaining cheese and either slip the dish under the broiler or use the kitchen torch to brown the cheese.

You can also prepare this dish a few hours ahead of time: Take it as far as transferring it to a serving vessel, then refrigerate. When needed, top with the cheese and warm in a preheated 350°F (180°C) oven until hot through. If the cheese does not brown enough in the oven, finish it under the broiler or with the kitchen torch.

1 lb (450 g) spinach

2 tablespoons unsalted butter

1 tablespoon diced yellow onion

¾ cup plus 2 tablespoons (200 ml) heavy cream

Salt and pepper

¾ cup (80 g) grated Gruyère or sharp Cheddar cheese

BONNIE
They gave me a leaflet saying Eat More Liver.

NURSE CRANE
I might give you one saying Eat More Eggs and Spinach.

SEASON 9: EPISODE 8

MOLDED MASH

Potatoes have been a cheap, filling food for the masses since their introduction to the United Kingdom in the mid-late seventeenth century. They caught on properly in the eighteenth century though, and by the end of the 1700s, they were being enthusiastically consumed in myriad ways, sometimes even turning up in sweet puddings. The British love affair with potatoes has been a deep one ever since, surviving both the horrors of the Irish Potato Famine, during which millions starved or emigrated in desperation, and the years of wartime rationing, when they were used as bulk in everything from mock meat loaf to scones and pastry. Often foods that were so associated with wartime went through a period of decline afterward, but not the humble spud. This recipe, which Shelagh serves to her family as part of a celebratory meal, is essentially the French pommes duchesse. *But molded mash is a bit more down to earth, in keeping with the context in which it is served.*

SERVES 4–6 AS A SIDE

Put the whole, skin-on potatoes in a large pan of salted water and bring to a boil over high heat. Boil until tender; the timing will depend on the size of your potatoes. Drain and leave to steam in the pan.

When the potatoes are cool enough to handle, rub off the skins and compost the skins for your allotment (!). Return the still-warm potatoes to the pan and mash them with a masher with the butter, which should melt when you add it. Alternatively, pass the still-warm unpeeled potatoes through a ricer into the pan and work in the butter with a fork. The potatoes should be very smooth and lump-free. Do not overwork. (Never use a food processor to mash them or you will have glue.) Now mix in the egg yolk. Season with salt (if needed) and pepper and the nutmeg. The mixture should be thick enough to pull away from the sides of the pan.

Line a large sheet pan with parchment paper or a silicone baking mat. Spoon the potato mixture into a piping bag fitted with a large star tip. Pipe 16–20 mounds of potato, each about 2 inches (5 cm) in diameter, twisting the tip and pressing down slightly as you finish to ensure a clean top that doesn't stick up too high. Chill the potato mounds for at least 30 minutes or up to 1 hour. About 15 minutes before baking, preheat the oven to 425°F (220°C).

In a small bowl, whisk together the whole egg with a pinch of salt to make an egg wash. (You won't need all of it, so this is an idea for how to use the half egg left over from making Melting Moments on page 74.) Brush each mound with the egg wash (gently, so as not to break the fluting).

Bake until golden brown and hot through, 15–20 minutes. Serve hot.

1 lb (450 g) baking potatoes

2 tablespoons butter, at room temperature

1 egg yolk, plus 1 whole egg, for egg wash

Salt and pepper

Generous pinch of ground nutmeg

TRIXIE
I'm sorry, but this is a completely dreadful way to convalesce! We're all dressed up as if we've burgled a jumble sale, and now we're peeling our own potatoes. Ugh!

SEASON 9: CHRISTMAS

BUTTERED CARROTS

The bright orange of a carrot side dish is a frequent sight on the tables of Call the Midwife. *It's a practical solution to a problem that crops up surprisingly often when filming food scenes, which is that an awful lot of food is brown or beige. Greens help to enliven matters, whether in the form of salad or beans, but a good bit of orange is also helpful. Fresh vegetables were widely eaten—we regularly see the street market in Poplar with its greengrocer stall—and allotments were a good way to grow your own for the many people living in flats or terraces with very limited outdoor space. However, a lot of urban people, in particular, lived mainly off canned fruit and vegetables, and even when fresh were around, they were supplemented with canned goods, especially in early spring. Canned goods only need reheating (if that), making them ideal for time-pressed families with little money for fuel. But if you do fancy a fresh carrot, then here you are. It's an ideal way to use carrots from the allotment when the patch needs to be thinned, but you could also use larger carrots cut into uniform pieces; aim for about 2 inches (5 cm) long.*

SERVES 4 AS A SIDE

Scrub the carrots well (if using older carrots, peel them) and trim the tops and tails. Put them in a high-sided frying pan with a lid. Add the butter and sugar and just enough water to cover the carrots. Place over medium-high heat and bring to a boil. Cover and reduce the heat to a simmer.

After about 4–6 minutes, the carrots should be softening but still resistant in the middle. Remove the lid, raise the heat to medium-high, and boil off the water. As the level reduces, turn the carrots to coat them in the remaining pan juices.

When the pan juices have disappeared, the carrots should be slightly wrinkled and shiny from the sugar-butter glaze. Serve at once, lightly sprinkled with salt and pepper if desired.

1¼ lb (570 g) baby carrots

4 tablespoons (60 g) butter

1½ teaspoons superfine sugar

Flaky sea salt and pepper (optional)

JENNY
I needed your advice. On what to grow. Because there's so much choice. Carrots obviously are helpful . . . but also cauliflower is delicious. Do we grow onions?

SISTER BERNADETTE
Oh, please stop wittering about vegetables, I could not care less.

SEASON 1: EPISODE 3

CAULIFLOWER WITH MINT SAUCE

Cauliflower has been around in Britain for over four hundred years. It was one of the staples of the winter table, usually served plain boiled but also the basis for cauliflower cheese (briefly boiled, smothered in béchamel sauce, and topped with cheese before being baked). In Call the Midwife, *it's often in the background, sometimes not entirely intentionally. Writer Heidi Thomas recalls an incident when she was viewing the rushes (the raw footage from each shoot) and spotted a plate of broccoli on a table. Broccoli was around in the 1950s, but only the sprouting kind, not the large-headed stuff we sometimes see today. And even the small stuff wouldn't have been common in Poplar. The solution? Fade out the color in postproduction so that what appeared on-screen looked, at least in passing, like cauliflower.*

This recipe is a suggestion from one of the increasing number of vegetarian cookery books published in the 1960s. If you are being strictly historically accurate, you should boil the cauliflower florets rather than roasting them—after spending a lot of time picking out caterpillars if The Home Book of Vegetarian Cookery *is to be believed. However, roasted cauli is a lot nicer.*

SERVES 4 AS A SIDE

In a small saucepan, combine the vinegar and sugar over medium heat and bring to a boil, stirring to dissolve the sugar. Remove from the heat and let cool. Put the mint into a bowl, pour the cooled vinegar mixture over the top, and set aside to steep for 2–3 hours.

Preheat the oven to 400°F (200°C). Remove the outer leaves from the cauliflower (see below). Cut or tear the cauliflower into uniform-size florets (2 inches/5 cm is a good size). Pile them on a large sheet pan, drizzle with the oil, and toss to coat evenly. Spread the florets in a single layer and sprinkle with the salt.

Roast the florets, turning them once at the halfway point, until tender when pierced with a fork, about 20 minutes. Transfer to a warmed serving plate and serve at once with the mint sauce on the side. You can cook and eat the outer leaves of the cauliflower, too, though they are best steamed and served around the florets.

1¼ cups (300 ml) white wine vinegar

3–4 tablespoons sugar

½ cup (30 g) finely chopped fresh mint

1 large cauliflower

¼ cup neutral vegetable oil

2 teaspoons coarse sea salt

FRED
Left some veg for you on the counter there, too. Cauliflowers and cabbages don't agree with my digestive system.

SEASON 11: EPISODE 2

BREAKFAST

In the first season of *Call the Midwife*, Fred buys a pig, declaring, "Bacon. It's the future." Two years later, the National Food Survey of 1958 showed he was right—sort of. Just four years after meat rationing ended, a cooked breakfast was eaten by half the population. Eggs, bacon, toast, and oodles of butter did feature on a lot of tables, but breakfast was just as likely to be eaten in a café as it was at home, and the cooked breakfast was often more of an aspiration than a reality.

The nurses and nuns of Nonnatus House do, usually, have a cooked meal in the morning. In season 3, Fred prepares a full fry-up for himself, but he offers it to Jenny, who is distraught after visiting Alec in hospital. In later episodes, we see the residents of the nunnery gathered around the breakfast table laden with bacon, toast, and eggs, while Fred feasts on bacon butties made by Violet—and Dr. Turner sneaks them from a local shop.

But the world was changing. Before the war, even relatively modest middle-class families had help at home, often a daily charwoman or a cook-general, who could prepare eggs and bacon to order. Now servants were in short supply, and the harried housewife rarely had time to prepare a full meal. Nor did her husband or children always have time to eat it. Shelagh experiments with Scotch pancakes on a semi-regular basis, but she has an electric food mixer to help. She also has extra motivation in her determination to create a home for a family she acknowledges is complicated, but one whose close bonds and happiness are vital to the balance of the series.

For those who didn't have a cooked breakfast, the standard breakfast in the 1950s was toast. For the wealthy, it was with butter, marmalade, and fruit preserves, while for the working classes, which make up the vast majority of the characters in *Call the Midwife*, it was with margarine, treacle, or condensed milk. Porridge was also popular, fueling around 20 percent of the working class—aided by the adoption of quick or instant oats, which had steadily gained ground since their invention in the early 1920s.

The biggest change over the period was the rise of breakfast cereals. They'd been introduced between the wars, emerging out of the American health food movement and originally seen as crank food. But they were easy and, in the 1950s, marketed hard at children. They carried a vague whiff of health about them, especially those based on fiber. Chummy eats bran flakes, while Sister Evangelina (reluctantly) chews on All-Bran. In the two decades following 1956, consumption of proprietary cereals doubled from 20 to 40 percent. Meanwhile, even the meal itself was under threat, from being almost universal in the 1950s to something that around 17 percent of the population skipped in the 1970s.

> **SISTER EVANGELINA**
> *If Nurse Gilbert wants my All-Bran when she arrives, she is more than welcome to it. It's like trying to digest a coconut mat.*
> SEASON 4: EPISODE 1

COLD
COLLATIONS

NURSE CRANE

I've never found grief and a cold spread to be an easy combination. The service itself is trial enough.

SEASON 7: EPISODE 8

QUICHE LORRAINE

Quiche Lorraine is really just a cheese and bacon flan with a more specific name. Flans have medieval origins as savory custards (the word custard *comes from the medieval croustade, which was a type of pie or tart). In the 1920s, the term* quiche *came into use, specifically for a flan with a base of cream and egg that also usually contained cheese and very often bacon. It probably comes from a dialect term in use in what is now the French department of Lorraine. By the 1920s, it was being referred to as quiche Lorraine. It's one of the staples of the Nonnatus House cold collation, served up after the afternoon clinics and before the evening duties start. It can also be served hot. Even by the 1960s, cooks were fiddling with the fillings, so feel free to swap the bacon for smoked salmon or add in some caramelized onions.*

SERVES 4 AS A MAIN COURSE OR 6–8 AS PART OF A BUFFET

To make the pastry, put the flour into a bowl and scatter the butter over the top. Using a pastry blender, cut the butter into the flour until the butter is in pieces the size of small peas. Drizzle the egg and 1 tablespoon of the water over the flour mixture and, using as few strokes as possible, stir and toss with a fork, adding just enough additional water, a little at a time, as needed for the dough to come together in a shaggy mass. Do not overwork. (This is easiest done in a food processor, first pulsing the butter into the flour and then pulsing in the egg and water.) Gently knead the dough in the bowl just enough to bring it together in a thick disk, then cover the bowl with a plate and refrigerate the dough for 30 minutes. Divide the dough in half and gently shape each half into a thick disk. Wrap 1 disk in plastic wrap and refrigerate for up to 1 day or freeze for up to 1 month for another use. Cover the second disk and refrigerate for 30 minutes.

Butter an 9-inch (23-cm) round flan (tart) pan or dish. On a lightly floured work surface, roll out the pastry into a round at least 11 inches (28 cm) in diameter and a scant 1/8 inch (3 mm) thick. Line the prepared pan with the pastry, leaving a slight overhang. Prick the bottom all over with fork tines. Line the pastry-lined pan with parchment paper and fill with dried beans or pie weights. Chill for another 30–45 minutes. Preheat the oven to 375°F (190°C).

Bake the pastry for 10 minutes. Carefully remove the beans and foil, and trim off the pastry overhang even with the rim. Continue to bake until the pastry is lightly cooked, about 15 minutes.

FOR THE PASTRY

1¾ cups plus 1 tablespoon (225 g) flour, plus more for the work surface

½ cup (115 g) cold butter, plus more for the pan

1 egg, lightly beaten

1–2 tablespoons ice-cold water

FOR THE FILLING

1 tablespoon butter

6 oz (170 g) white button mushrooms, brushed clean and diced

8 slices bacon, chopped

1 cup (115 g) mixed grated sharp Cheddar and Gruyère or Emmentaler cheese, in equal parts, or all Cheddar

2/3 cup (160 ml) heavy cream or half-and-half

3 egg yolks

Pepper

Recipe continues on the following page

Continued from the previous page

While the crust is baking, make the filling. In a frying pan, melt the butter over medium heat. Add the mushrooms and bacon, and cook, stirring occasionally, until the bacon starts to crisp and the mushrooms yield their water, about 5 minutes. Remove from the heat.

In a bowl, whisk together the cheese, cream, and egg yolks until well blended. Season generously with pepper. Add the bacon and mushrooms, and mix well.

Remove the crust from the oven and carefully pour the filling into it. Return the pan to the oven, reduce the oven temperature to 325°F (165°C), and bake until a knife inserted near the center comes out clean, about 30 minutes. Let cool on a wire rack before serving.

SISTER EVANGELINA
What is this?

SISTER WINIFRED
It's called "Quiche Lorraine," according to Mrs. B.

SISTER EVANGELINA
Pass me the beetroot. With Sister Julienne's permission, I'll make myself a sandwich.

SEASON 3: EPISODE 5

CHEESE AND TOMATO TARTLETS

One of the other staples at the early evening cold collation is cheese tarts or cheese and tomato tarts. When Nurse Phyllis Crane arrives in season 4, she makes her mark immediately with her car and her vegetarianism—unusual in the 1960s. However, as the years move on, we meet other vegetarians, and her own meat-free habits become less eye-opening to the rest of Nonnatus House. The British cheese industry had been very badly affected by the restrictions of the Second World War, during which time cheese was virtually nationalized and only a few types allowed to be produced. As a result, most postwar recipes simply call for "cheese," meaning hard cheese of the Cheddar type. Happily, we are better off now, and wherever you are in the world, you should be able to find a good, well-rounded cheese to really make this dish sing. Some things have definitely improved since 1959.

MAKES 6 TARTLETS

To make the pastry, put the flour into a bowl and scatter the butter over the top. Using a pastry blender, cut the butter into the flour until the butter is in pieces the size of small peas. Drizzle 1–2 tablespoons of the water evenly over the flour mixture and, using as few strokes as possible, stir and toss with a fork, adding just enough additional water, a little at a time, as needed for the dough to come together in a shaggy mass. Do not overwork. (This is easiest done in a food processor, first pulsing the butter into the flour and then pulsing in the water.) Gently knead the dough in the bowl just enough to bring it together in a thick disk, then cover the bowl with a plate and refrigerate the dough for 30 minutes.

Butter six 3-inch (7.5-cm) round tartlet pans, preferably with removable bottoms. On a lightly floured work surface, roll out the pastry into a round a scant 1/8 inch (3 mm) thick. Using a round template about 1 inch (2.5 cm) larger than the diameter of a tartlet pan, cut out as many rounds as possible. Transfer each pastry round to a prepared tartlet pan, pressing it into the bottom and up the sides and using your fingers to "cut" away the excess. Gather up the dough scraps, press together, reroll, and cut out more rounds as needed to line all the prepared pans. Place the pastry-lined pans on a sheet pan and refrigerate for 30 minutes.

To make the béchamel, pour the milk into a small saucepan and heat over medium heat just until hot, then remove from the heat. While the milk is heating, in another small saucepan, melt the butter over medium heat. Sprinkle in the flour, then stir the butter and flour constantly with a wooden spoon until a paste forms. Add the hot milk, 1–2 tablespoons at a time, whisking or stirring well after each addition. Then continue to stir over medium heat until you have a fairly thick, smooth sauce. Season with salt and pepper and the nutmeg, and then set aside until tepid. Preheat the oven to 400°F (200°C).

Recipe continues on the following page

FOR THE PASTRY

¾ cup plus 2 tablespoons (110 g) flour, plus more for the work surface

4 tablespoons (60 g) cold butter, cut into small cubes, plus more for the pans

2–3 tablespoons ice-cold water

FOR THE BÉCHAMEL

½ cup (120 ml) milk

½ tablespoon butter

1 tablespoon flour

Salt and pepper

Pinch of ground nutmeg

FOR THE FILLING

2 oz (60 g) cream cheese, at room temperature

1 egg, separated

2 tablespoons grated sharp cheese, such as Cheddar, Gruyère, or Lincolnshire Poacher

Splash of Tabasco sauce

¼ cup (30 g) grated Parmesan cheese

1 ripe tomato, thinly sliced (6 slices)

Continued from the previous page

To make the filling, add the cream cheese, egg yolk, sharp cheese, and Tabasco to the béchamel and stir to mix. In a bowl, whisk the egg white until stiff peaks form. Gently fold the egg white into the béchamel mixture just until incorporated. Divide the filling evenly among the tartlet pans.

Bake the tartlets until the filling puffs up and is just set, 12–15 minutes. Remove from the oven and sprinkle each tartlet with 1 teaspoon of the Parmesan, then top with a tomato slice. Top the tomato slices with the remaining Parmesan, sprinkling 1 teaspoon on each slice. Return the tartlets to the oven and bake until the Parmesan is golden and bubbling, 12-15 minutes.

Let the tartlets cool on the sheet pan on a wire rack until they can be handled, then carefully remove the tartlets from the pans. Serve warm as part of a supper or at room temperature with a side salad and a huge pot of tea.

RECIPE NOTE Finishing each tartlet with a little green garnish, such as finely chopped fresh chives, thyme, or flat-leaf parsley, is a nice touch.

SISTER EVANGELINA
What's this?

SISTER WINIFRED
It's a cheese tart. Nurse Crane suggested it.

NURSE CRANE
You've had major surgery. Below the waist. You don't want to tax your digestion with animal matter.

SISTER EVANGELINA
Cheese is animal matter. And this is a quiche. You know my feelings.

SEASON 4: EPISODE 6

GREEN SALAD

Always present at the Nonnatus House cold collation is a large green salad. Sometimes it's plain, sometimes there are tomatoes, sometimes a hard-boiled egg or five. British salads shared some of the issues that dogged British vegetable cookery in the era: a lack of imagination, conservative view of ingredients, and a focus on meat above all else. But there were those who took up the challenge. In 1950, the delightful 282 Ways of Making a Salad *by Bebe Daniels and Jill Allgood promised to show the reader "how to make attractive, health-giving meals," lamenting the British tendency to rely on "tired lettuce leaves in company with wilting tomatoes and cucumber." They solicited recipes from celebrities in both Britain and America, with contributors including Vivien Leigh and Laurence Olivier, Gregory Peck, and Frank Sinatra. The results are mixed, with alarming numbers of the American Jell-O salads that thankfully failed to make much of an impact in Britain. There are some really good salads though, and dressing ideas. However, the book is as notable for its complete lack of impact as for any of the recipes. Nobody else's advice seemed to help either. This, then, is a plain salad but with a choice of two reliable dressings—about as good as it got.*

SERVES 4–6

Wash the salad leaves thoroughly and dry them in a salad spinner or by putting them in a large, dry kitchen towel and spinning them round your head. (According to one book, you can also dry the leaves by putting them in a salad basket and pinning it to the clothesline to let the wind do the work.)

Chop or tear the leaves into pieces small enough to eat with a degree of decorum. Peel the cucumber if it is a home-grown or bitter variety and cut it into ¼-inch (6-mm) cubes.

Put all the leaves, the cucumber, parsley, and chives into a large bowl. Add the salt and season well with pepper, then toss. Adorn the bowl with the hard-boiled eggs, if using.

½ head bitter lettuce, such as frisée or curly endive, or a small bunch of watercress

1 head Belgian endive

1 small head standard lettuce, such as iceberg or romaine

1 bunch leafy greens, such as mâche or baby spinach

½ cucumber

2 tablespoons minced fresh flat-leaf parsley

1 teaspoon minced fresh chives

2 teaspoons salt

Pepper

2 hard-boiled eggs, peeled and quartered lengthwise (optional)

Recipe continues on the following page

Continued from the previous page

If you opt for the French dressing, simply put all the ingredients into a clean, dry jam jar, put the lid on tightly, and shake. You can also put everything into a jug and use a whisk to mix them. The sauce should emulsify and form a smooth, creamy, and fairly thick pale-yellow liquid. Pour into a jug and serve this on the side of the salad for everyone to add as desired.

If you prefer the idea of salad cream, in a bowl, mash the egg yolks until very smooth. Add the mustard, salt, and pepper, and beat well. Add the oil, a dribble at a time, beating well to emulsify. Then add the cream in the same way. Finally, add the vinegar, again beating well to incorporate. Pour into a jug and serve immediately before it separates.

FOR THE FRENCH DRESSING

½ teaspoon salt

1 teaspoon Dijon mustard

1 tablespoon white wine vinegar

1 tablespoon tarragon vinegar

½ cup (120 ml) neutral vegetable oil, or 6 tablespoons (90 ml) neutral vegetable oil and 2 tablespoons fruity olive oil

FOR THE SALAD CREAM

2 hard-boiled egg yolks

1 teaspoon English mustard

½ teaspoon salt

½ teaspoon black pepper, or ¼ teaspoon cayenne pepper

¼ cup (60 ml) neutral vegetable oil

6 tablespoons (90 ml) heavy cream

1 tablespoon white wine vinegar

TRIXIE
You'll have to excuse me, I'm going to make myself a face mask out of salad cream. I believe one can find the most amazing aids to beauty in the kitchen cupboards.

SEASON 5: EPISODE 4

HERRING AND POTATO SALAD

A mainstay of the working class for centuries, preserved fish remained popular despite the availability of canned fish from the mid-nineteenth century onward. Preserved herring is usually associated with northern Europe and Ashkenazic Jewish cuisine. In season 4, the Jewish Polish family who appears in episode 3 enjoys schmaltz herring and pickled cucumbers. But herring was also widely eaten in the United Kingdom, though it was more generally smoked or pickled. Potato salad, meanwhile, was ubiquitous, and often included olives, pickled onion, or similarly strong flavors. This particular recipe appeared in a number of books from the 1930s onward and was based on Scandinavian salads. Beets (UK beetroots) are a common Nonnatus House addition, regularly appearing on the table for tea, and are seen in the Buckles' larder. In season 7, Magda reveals beet was used for rouge when she was at school behind the Iron Curtain.

SERVES 4–6

In a saucepan, combine the potatoes with salted water to cover and bring to a boil over high heat. Adjust the heat to a steady simmer and cook until tender but not falling apart, 10–15 minutes; the timing will depend on the size of your potatoes. Drain well and return to the pan to steam dry. You can serve this salad with the potatoes still warm, so don't worry about cooling them.

While the potatoes are cooking, drain the herring, reserving the oil. Chop the herring into large chunks. In a small bowl, mix 1 tablespoon of the reserved oil with the vinegar to create a dressing.

In a serving bowl, combine the herring, apple, beets, gherkins, olives, and onion, and toss well. Season with salt and pepper. Add the potatoes and turn them gently, being careful not to break them up. Drizzle with the dressing, turn gently to coat, and serve.

RECIPE TIP If you can't find herring in oil, use rollmops, which come in vinegar. Just trade out the tarragon vinegar and the oil from the herring in the recipe for a mild olive oil and add 1 teaspoon chopped fresh tarragon. You can also use dill or parsley.

1 lb (450 g) waxy potatoes, quartered

1 container (8 oz/225g) matjes herring in oil (4–6 herring fillets)

2 tablespoons tarragon vinegar

1 eating apple, such as Granny Smith, cored and diced

2 medium or 4 small pickled beets, diced

1 tablespoon chopped pickled gherkins or cucumber

About 10 black olives, pitted and halved

1 small pickled onion or 5–6 cocktail onions, roughly chopped

Salt and pepper

SISTER MONICA JOAN
Potato salad. Often a harbinger of doom.

SEASON 5:
EPISODE 3

SOME NOTES ON SANDWICHES

It would be impossible to list all the sandwiches consumed in *Call the Midwife*. Whether it's the Nonnatus House staff on call or their patients at work or at home, two slices of bread and a filling are the natural quick meal. We see them eaten on picnics, at a table, on benches, and on buses. They're usually wrapped in paper, but in typical *Call the Midwife* fashion, we see the march of time subtly unfold through the medium of sandwich containers. Chummy and, later, Fred, use Tupperware (the company was founded in the 1940s in America, expanding to Europe a decade or so later). Aluminium foil was invented in the Edwardian era but was mainly used in catering until the 1950s. By the 1960s, it had spread to homes, but it was sufficiently new and exciting that Bacofoil, which was founded in 1962, felt the need to employ television chef Fanny Cradock to extol its virtues and explain its uses in a 1967 cookery book. In it, she used foil not just for cooking but also as an integral part of dish presentation.

The sandwich itself is a very basic thing. The concept is undatable—it's hardly difficult to imagine putting a slice of ham or a chunk of cheese between slices of bread or into a pita— but the name dates to the eighteenth century. It was named for John Montagu, 4th Earl of Sandwich, a businessman apparently with a particular penchant for eating at his desk. Very quickly, the idea, and name, developed in a vast range of directions, from bite-size morsels for the aristocratic dinner party to a chunky bap wrapped around a meat patty—a burger, as it became known.

Naturally, the 1950s and 1960s produced their own sandwich-shaped ideas. The Danish open sandwich, made as colorful as possible, was promoted as a cool way to present nibbles at canapé parties. There were Swiss (jelly) roll–inspired sandwiches, in which a slightly flattened slice of bread was spread with a paste filling and then rolled up. Then there were riffs on the sausage roll formula: crusty baguettes stuffed not just with sausages or frankfurters but with anything of a similar shape, such as bananas. One author further suggested sandwich cones (bread shaped on a cream horn mold and then filled), playing card sandwiches (cut out with appropriately shaped cutters), and kebabs "in blankets," a sort of bread hammock folded halfway around the kebab (still on its skewer, so slightly challenging to eat).

The suggestions here are mainly from the show and less alarming than those in many of the books of the time. However, don't let common sense or good taste stop you from trying out the final showstopper.

All sandwiches should use good bread. Whether it is white or brown is up to you. In the 1950s and 1960s, white was almost universal except for folks on health kicks. With the exception of the first two suggestions, they also benefit from spreading lots of salted butter on the bread. And don't forget that sandwiches need seasoning, too. The vast majority of sandwich ingredients would have been purchased from a grocer or butcher, though I've included a recipe for potting your own leftovers should you want to give it a try.

VEGETARIAN

Sweetened condensed milk (yes, really), then fry the sandwich in butter until golden on both sides
Golden syrup and clotted cream, known as "thunder and lightning" and popular in the West Country; add a little cocoa powder to boost things even further
Grated Cheddar cheese (grating helps the cheese stay in the sandwich)
Red Leicester cheese and radish slices
Fried egg with a dash of Tabasco sauce
Hard-boiled egg and mayonnaise (anchovy was also often added by nonvegetarians)

MEAT AND FISH

Banana and bacon
Lots of bacon
Salmon (tinned rather than smoked)
Corned beef (mashing it with butter helps it stay in place)
Ham and piccalilli
Spam and pickle (better if you fry the Spam first)

Make Your Own Filling If you fancy making potted beef sandwiches, which appear in season 7, episode 5, it's very easy. Simply take leftover roast beef and pound it in a mortar with a pestle (or blitz it in a food processor) along with one-fourth its weight in butter and a generous amount of ground mace, white pepper, cayenne pepper, and salt. Press the resulting purée into a jar and cover with a layer of clarified butter about 1/2 inch (12 mm) thick. You can apply this technique to almost any meat. You can also do the same with cheese, though it is worth adding a little white wine to the mixture to loosen it to spreading consistency.

Another easy sandwich filling is flavored butter, which is made by adding herbs, spices, or other flavorings to butter. Simply process room-temperature butter in a blender or food processor with the flavoring of your choice until light and creamy. For each 1/2 cup (115 g) butter, use 2 oil-packed anchovy fillets for anchovy butter or 4 teaspoons minced fresh chives for chive butter. Marmite or similar highly savory spreads also work well. Use 2–3 teaspoons Marmite for each 1/2 cup (115 g) butter, making sure the butter is unsalted.

A GIANT SANDWICH LOAF

Several authors believe this outsized sandwich is ideal for picnics or serious entertaining. It is, at least, a talking point.

SERVES 4–6

Trim off all the crusts from the loaf to create a uniform rectangle. Using a serrated knife, cut the loaf horizontally into four equal slices. Spread each slice first with butter and then with a different filling of your choice. For maximum effect, go for contrasting colors but complementary flavors, such as ham with mustard, egg with mayonnaise, watercress with cottage cheese, and puréed chicken with almonds and a little cream.

Put the loaf back together and spread the top, sides, and ends with the cream cheese. Chill about 5 minutes. Decorate in a suitably exuberant fashion, such as flowers made from apple petals, olive centers, and gherkin stems or from radish slices with gherkin centers, coiled carrot ribbons, scallop shapes cut from sliced tomato, celery leaves, and chives and herb sprig stems. Cut into slices to serve.

1 small loaf sandwich bread (pullman loaf)

Butter, at room temperature

Fillings, to taste (a loaded term)

8 oz (225 g) cream cheese, at room temperature

Decorations of choice, such as thinly sliced radishes, apples, tomato, celery, and gherkins; carrot ribbons; black and green olives; and fresh chives and herb sprigs

DRINKS

Call the Midwife runs on tea. It's effectively still the British national drink, and Britain has been known as a nation of tea drinkers since the middle of the eighteenth century, when tea was still very expensive and the vast majority was smuggled to avoid tax. The 1958 National Food Survey showed that people averaged six cups a day, starting when they woke around seven and ending with supper around nine. Almost everyone drank it with sugar and milk. We see the milkman do his rounds in many episodes of *Call the Midwife*, and also see the consternation when the milk can't be delivered due to a lack of bottles during the Big Freeze of 1963–64 (season 7). However, with no refrigeration in most homes, and fresh milk often prioritized for children, many Poplar residents used long-life milks in their tea. The real Jenny Lee recalled in her memoir that she learned to decline her patients' offers of tea for it was "revolting: strong enough to creosote a fence, stewed for hours, and laced with sticky sweet condensed milk." Most people used leaf tea. Bags had been launched in 1952 but were slow to catch on until the 1970s.

Coffee was another option, both as instant granules and, somewhat skewed toward the wealthy, made with ground coffee. The Turners have a moka pot, invented by Bialetti in 1933. Meanwhile, in season 7, Rhoda Mullocks shares a moment with a fellow mother of a thalidomide-affected baby over coffee brewed in her Cona coffee maker. In the late 1950s, there was also a brief vogue for Italian coffee shops, all gleaming Gaggia machines and teeny espressos.

Another hot drink frequently mentioned in the show is Horlicks, a malt-based beverage made with milk. It was one of several drinks marketed originally as health drinks. Horlicks was apparently good to stave off "night starvation," a concept entirely invented by the company itself. Bournvita, which Barbara drinks, was malt and chocolate, as was Ovaltine, enjoyed by Delia in season 6.

Beyond hot drinks, we also see a range of cooling beverages, many of which, again, were originally conceived of as health drinks. Even lemonade, which was being drunk by at least the seventeenth century, was seen as a way to refresh the spirit and further good health. Nurse Crane, meanwhile, enjoys barley water, originally made by boiling barley with water and used to lubricate sore throats, while Fred usually has a bottle or two of Dandelion & Burdock—a root-based drink much promoted by the temperance movement in the nineteenth century—on hand.

PATSY

Apart from our cocktail of the day, which is the Grasshopper: equal parts creme de menthe, creme de cacao, evap, and a dash of cocoa. Slips down like a liquid after-dinner mint and then kicks you like a mule.

SEASON 6: EPISODE 1

There are, of course, alcoholic drinks as well, though fewer after Trixie's acknowledgment of her alcoholism and subsequent journey to sobriety. Beer was ubiquitous, and we see it in pubs and at home with the Buckles and the Turners. Wine was less common, though increasing in popularity, partly due to good marketing from the likes of Blue Nun. Jenny's preferred tipple is Babycham, a sparkling perry that enjoyed a huge following at the time. Then there are port and lemon, Scotch and Canada Dry (ginger ale), and enough sherry—Tio Pepe, El Cid—to float a canal boat. Advocaat, described by Trixie as "a naughty version of eggnog," is a Dutch alcoholic beverage that tastes a lot like brandy custard sauce. It's the basis of the snowball, a popular Christmastime cocktail made with lemonade and lime. In season 6, the nurses frequently gather around Trixie's drinks shelf and make cocktails drawn from the pages of *Woman's Realm*. Some, like the brandy Alexander, are familiar, if old-fashioned, today. Others, such as the evaporated milk–based grasshopper, are more alarming. The latter was normally made with cream; the evaporated milk gives it that special 1960s *Call the Midwife* twist.

SWEETS

SISTER JULIENNE

One way or another, you will be sent home to convalesce. It's simply a case of who gets to eat the pudding.

SEASON 2: EPISODE 5

TREACLE SPONGE

Treacle sponge (or treacle sponge pudding) was a late-Victorian specialty that had a dual life as a nursery favorite for wealthy families and a midweek easy pudding for workers. It's pure comfort food in both cases, and it's not surprising that both Chummy and Peter Noakes love it despite their different backgrounds. Steaming it makes for a very moist cake, while the suet keeps it light and fluffy. It can also be made in a pressure cooker, which was a very popular kitchen gadget in the late 1960s, in which case steam without pressure for 20 minutes and then on low pressure for 35 minutes.

SERVES 6—8

Butter a 2½-cup (600-ml) pudding mold. Cut a round of parchment paper and a round of aluminum foil about 3 inches (7.5 cm) larger than the top of the mold. Butter one side of the parchment.

In a bowl, combine the flour, bread crumbs, currants, suet, sugar, ginger, baking powder, and salt, and stir until well mixed. Add the egg, golden syrup, and ½ cup (120 ml) of the water, and stir until well mixed, adding a little more water if needed to create a thick batter. It should not be too liquid.

Pour the batter into the prepared mold. Place the parchment round, buttered side down, on the mold and top with the foil round. Make a narrow pleat across the center of the layered rounds (this will allow the pudding to rise as it steams), press the overhang down the sides of the mold, and tie the rounds tightly in place around the rim of the mold with kitchen string. To make a handle to ease lowering and lifting the mold, thread the end of a long length of string under the string on one side of the mold, then thread the other end under the string on the opposite side. Bring the ends together and tie securely, leaving enough slack for the pudding to rise.

Select a saucepan large enough to accommodate the mold with room for circulating steam. Place a trivet or an inverted heatproof saucer on the bottom of the pan and fill the pan with water to reach about halfway up the sides of the mold once it is added. Bring the water to a boil over high heat and carefully lower the mold into the pan. Let the water return to a full boil, then cover the pan and lower the heat so the water is still bubbling but not so vigorously that it splashes over the top of the pudding.

Steam for 2½ hours, topping up the water with boiling water as necessary to maintain the original level. The pudding is done when a skewer inserted into the center comes out with no more than a few moist crumbs.

Turn off the heat, carefully lift the pudding mold from the water, and set it on a wire rack. Snip the string, remove the foil and parchment, and allow the pudding to cool in the mold on the rack for 10–15 minutes. Use a blunt knife to loosen the edges of the pudding from the mold, then invert a serving plate on top of the mold, invert the plate and mold together, and lift off the mold.

Butter, for the mold

1 cup (125 g) flour

1 cup (40 g) fresh bread crumbs

⅔ cup (110 g) dried currants

1 cup (115 g) shredded suet

1 tablespoon sugar

1 teaspoon ground ginger

1 teaspoon baking powder

½ teaspoon salt

1 egg, lightly beaten

¾ cup (250 g) golden syrup

½–1 cup (120–240 ml) water

1 pint (480 ml) vanilla ice cream or hot custard (see Recipe Note), for serving

You can serve this pudding hot, in which case vanilla ice cream is an excellent accompaniment, or cold, in which case hot custard is best.

RECIPE NOTE You can serve this pudding with hot custard made from store bought custard powder (Bird's is the most popular brand; see 1960s Spin, page 164), but for a slightly more sophisticated twist, make your custard sauce from scratch: In a saucepan, warm 2½ cups (600 ml) milk over medium heat just to a simmer. Meanwhile, in a bowl, whisk together 3 eggs yolks, ¼ cup (60 ml) syrup from a jar of stem ginger, and 2½ tablespoons cornstarch or custard powder until pale yellow. Remove the milk from the heat and begin adding the milk to the egg yolk mixture, a few tablespoons at a time, while whisking constantly. When about half of the milk has been incorporated, slowly pour in the remaining milk while whisking constantly. Then pour the mixture back into the saucepan and heat over low heat, stirring constantly, until the sauce thickens and coats the back of spoon. If you replace the currants in the sponge with chopped stem ginger as well, you've transformed a nursery pudding into a dinner-party winner.

P.C. NOAKES
I've just found out I have to pass a physical examination. I've never been a stranger to a treacle sponge. Married life's only made me more accustomed. I get out of puff when I do the stairs. I might not pass.

SEASON 2:
EPISODE 2

BREAD AND BUTTER PUDDING

An incredibly simple recipe that is satisfyingly stodgy and really good at using up slightly stale bread, this is another Victorian staple that stood (and stands) the test of time. Leftovers today are regarded as a bit low grade, but that wasn't as true in the 1950s, when items left from one meal were simply useful ingredients to make up the next. Bread, which is one of the most wasted foods in the twenty-first century, was used for bread crumbs, double baked to make crackers, put into stuffings and meatballs, and made into puddings like this one. Trixie feeds bread pudding to a sloshed Barbara in season 1, and there's no doubting its usefulness in lining the stomach. It's very forgiving to cook, and while this recipe uses a flattish pie dish, you can also make it in a deep-sided dish or indeed a pudding mold. It can also be steamed as well as baked.

SERVES 6

Butter a 9½-inch (24-cm) pie dish.

Spread each slice of bread fairly thickly with butter and then with jam. Lay them, jam side up, in two or more layers in the prepared pie dish. In a bowl, whisk together the milk, eggs, sugar, and vanilla until blended. Pour the mixture over the bread. Let soak for 30–45 minutes. About 15 minutes before the soak is finished, preheat the oven to 350°F (180°C).

Sprinkle the top of the pudding with a little sugar. Bake the pudding until the custard has set and the top is golden brown and crispy, 35–40 minutes.

Remove the pudding from the oven and serve it hot or cold. If it is hot, it is good with ice cream or cream; if it is cold, it is good with (yet more) hot custard.

RECIPE NOTE You can leave off the jam or marmalade and instead sprinkle a few tablespoons of dried currants, first briefly rehydrated in boiling water, between the bread layers.

6–8 thin slices white sandwich bread (pullman loaf)

5 tablespoons (75 g) butter, for the pie dish and for the bread

4–5 tablespoons (80–100 g) jam or marmalade of choice

3¾ cups (900 ml) milk

3 eggs

2 tablespoons sugar, plus more for sprinkling

2 teaspoons pure vanilla extract

Ice cream or heavy cream if serving hot, or hot custard if serving cold

LEMON MERINGUE PIE

One of a number of iconic desserts of the late twentieth century, lemon meringue pie (or tart) has slipped from modern menus but not from modern consciousness. It has a significant walk-on role in season 3 of Call the Midwife, *when a particularly cloudlike specimen disappears from Nonnatus House, one of a series of thefts that result in the police being called out. The denouement, which revolves around Sister Evangelina and her backstory, is characteristically poignant. However, it does mean no one at Nonnatus House gets to eat the tart. Recipes abounded in books of the time, and everyone seemed to have a version. One Belfast school even managed to get a recipe from Bob Hope for its charity cookbook. The filling was usually lemon juice, sugar, and cornstarch, but by the 1960s, you could easily buy a ready-made version, making the pie even simpler to prepare. Rather than fully echo those fillings, this recipe takes a step back, for it's based on an eighteenth century lemon pudding recipe, essentially a lemon curd in pastry. It reflects the flavors of the Victorian era, a period we sometimes forget is still very much part of life in the 1950s: The older characters were born during Victoria's reign, and some of them, especially Sister Monica Joan with her wealthy background, would have been brought up very much with the food of that earlier era. Amid the riot of food coloring and silver balls, it's sometimes salutary to remember the food of the decades that went before.*

SERVES 8

To make the pastry in a bowl, stir together the flour and superfine sugar. Add the butter and, using a pastry blender, cut the butter into the flour mixture until the butter is in pieces the size of small peas. Drizzle the egg and 1 tablespoon of the water over the flour mixture and, using as few strokes as possible, stir and toss until the dough comes together in a rough mass, adding a little more water if needed to bring the pastry together. (This is easiest done in a food processor, first pulsing the butter into the flour-sugar mixture and then pulsing in the egg and water.) Do not overwork. Divide the dough in half and gently shape each half into a thick disk in the bowl. Wrap 1 disk in plastic wrap and refrigerate for up to 1 day or freeze for up to 1 month for another use. Leave the second disk in the bowl, cover the bowl with a plate, and refrigerate the dough for 30 minutes.

Butter an 9-inch (23-cm) pie tin or tart pan with a removable bottom. On a lightly floured work surface, roll out the pastry into a round about 11 inches (28 cm) in diameter and a scant ⅛ inch (3 mm) thick. Line the prepared pan with the pastry, allowing the excess to drape over the sides. Using a small knife, trim the edges, leaving a ½-inch (12-mm) overhang, then roll the overhang back over itself and press against the sides of the pan. Line the pastry-lined pan with aluminum foil or parchment paper and fill with dried beans or pie weights. Chill for another 30 minutes. Preheat the oven to 325°F (165°C).

FOR THE PASTRY

1¾ cups plus 1 tablespoon (225 g) flour, plus more for the work surface

1 tablespoon superfine sugar

½ cup (115 g) cold butter, cut into small cubes, plus more for the pan

1 egg, lightly beaten

1–2 tablespoons ice-cold water

FOR THE LEMON CURD

Zest and juice of 2 lemons

1 cup (225 g) unsalted butter, at room temperature

1 cup plus 2 tablespoons (225 g) superfine sugar

3 egg yolks

Bake the pastry for 20 minutes on a baking sheet lined with parchment paper. Carefully remove the beans and foil, and continue to bake until the pastry is golden brown and fully cooked, 15–20 minutes longer. Let cool completely on a wire rack

To make the lemon curd, peel the lemons, removing as little of the white pith with the peel as possible. In a small saucepan, combine the lemon peels with water to cover, bring to a gentle boil over medium-high heat, and "stew" the peels until tender, 30–45 minutes; the timing will depend on the thickness of the peels. Drain well.

In a blender or food processor, purée the lemon peels, gradually adding the lemon juice, butter, granulated sugar, and egg yolks. Continue to purée until the mixture is thick and creamy, 3–5 minutes. Transfer the mixture to a small saucepan over low heat (if you are a confident custard maker) or to a heatproof bowl set over (not touching) simmering water in a saucepan and heat gently, stirring continuously. Do not let it boil. Cook until the mixture reaches 170°F (77°C) on an instant-read thermometer and thickens to the consistency of thick custard, 10–12 minutes. Remove from the heat, cover, and let cool completely. The curd will thicken as it cools.

You've now got the makings of a lemon curd tart. Just pour the curd into the cooled tart shell and smooth the top. Chill until you are ready to top it with the meringue, which can be done shortly before serving. If you aren't keen on the meringue layer, now is the time to stop, though if you decide to serve it plain, it benefits from 10 minutes in a 400°F (200°C) oven to brown the top.

When you're ready to make the meringue, preheat the oven to 350°F (180°C). In a bowl, whisk the egg whites with the cream of tartar until they start to foam. Add the superfine sugar in three lots, beating well after each addition. When the whites form soft peaks, add the confectioners' sugar and whisk until stiff peaks form.

Dollop this meringue mixture generously on top of the lemon curd, covering it completely. Bake until the meringue is hard to the touch and brown on top but squidgy and soft underneath, about 10 minutes. Let cool completely on a wire rack. If using a tart pan, carefully unmold the tart from the tart pan, first removing the outer ring and then gently sliding the tart off the pan bottom onto a serving plate.

FOR THE MERINGUE (OPTIONAL)

3 egg whites

Pinch of cream of tartar

¾ cup plus 1½ tablespoons (170 g) superfine sugar

⅔ cup (80 g) confectioners' sugar

PATSY
Oh, Lord! Is that lemon meringue pie?

CHUMMY
Oh, sorry, old thing. It's spoken for. It's been promised as a raffle prize.

SEASON 3: EPISODE 5

BANANA CORONET

One of the more memorable sweets in Call the Midwife, *banana coronet never appears on-screen in its completed form but does feature as a printed recipe in season 3 when Trixie and the other nurses are planning Sister Evangelina's jubilee celebration. The image of the recipe we see on-screen was mocked up specially for the show, but it's based on contemporary banana cake recipes with a visual twist. This is remarked upon in plain terms by Nurse Patsy Mount, newly arrived at Nonnatus House from working on the male surgical ward and with an earthy sense of humor not entirely in keeping with the sometimes more rarefied atmosphere of what is, after all, a nunnery. Given it's a celebration cake, it's worth cracking out a fancy cake mold, if you have one. A* Kugelhopf *or Bundt pan is ideal. Otherwise, the original recipe simply calls for a plain round pan. You may need to adjust the cooking time depending on the design of your pan, so it's worth checking the cake after 45 minutes and keeping an eye on it after that.*

SERVES 8

To make the cake, preheat the oven to 350°F (180°C). Butter the bottom and sides of an 8-inch (20-cm) round cake pan (see headnote), then sprinkle with superfine sugar, tapping out the excess. The sugar will help the cake develop a good crust.

Sift together the flour, baking powder, and baking soda into a medium bowl. In a large bowl, using an electric mixer, beat together the butter and superfine sugar on medium speed until the mixture is light in color and fluffy. Add the eggs, one at a time, along with a tablespoon of the flour mixture with each egg to prevent the mixture from curdling, beating well after each addition. Add the vanilla and beat until mixed. On low speed, add the flour mixture in three batches alternately with the milk in two batches, beginning and ending with the flour mixture and mixing well after each addition. Finally, add the bananas and mix well. The mixture will be lumpy with banana, and that's fine. Transfer the batter to the prepared pan.

Bake the cake until a skewer inserted into the center comes out clean, 1–1½ hours. The timing will vary depending on the shape of the pan. Let cool in the pan on a wire rack for 30 minutes, then turn the cake out onto the rack and let cool completely.

When you are ready to assemble the cake, make the buttercream. In a bowl, combine the butter, banana, and lemon juice. Sift the confectioners' sugar into the bowl, then beat together all the ingredients until you have a smooth, slightly runny mixture. Cover and chill to spreading consistency, about 30 minutes.

FOR THE CAKE

6 tablespoons (90 g) butter, plus more for the pan

1 cup plus 2 tablespoons (225 g) superfine sugar, plus more for the pan

2¾ cups (350 g) flour

½ teaspoon baking powder

½ teaspoon baking soda

2 eggs

½ teaspoon pure vanilla extract

6 tablespoons (90 ml) milk

2 very ripe bananas, peeled and mashed

FOR THE BUTTERCREAM

3 tablespoons butter, at room temperature

1 ripe banana, peeled and mashed

½ teaspoon fresh lemon juice

2½ cups (300 g) confectioners' sugar

TO FINISH

4–6 good-looking bananas

Glacé cherries and candied angelica (optional)

Recipe continues on the following page

Continued from the previous page

If the cake has domed in the oven, trim with a serrated knife so the top is flat. Set the cake on a large plate and cover the top and sides with the buttercream, leaving a little buttercream aside for sticking on the bananas. If you are not serving immediately, stop here.

Peel the bananas and cut them in half lengthwise and then crosswise. Use the reserved buttercream to stick the bananas perkily around the sides of the cake (you may find a judicious use of cocktail sticks necessary if the bananas start to slip). Decorate the center of the cake with cherries and angelica, if using. Serve the cake within a few hours, before the bananas go brown.

TRIXIE
It's called a Banana Coronet.

PATSY
It looks a bit like Stonehenge, only made of penises.

SEASON 3:
EPISODE 5

QUEEN OF PUDDINGS

Queen of puddings seems to have evolved out of a number of similar puddings in the late nineteenth century, including one called Aunt Louisa's pudding, which used apricot jam in place of the strawberry. It's a cheap and easy way to turn custard into an approximation of a sponge, and it's very versatile, as it can be served hot, cold, or somewhere in between. By the 1960s, it was a family dish, especially aimed at children who could cope with its incredible sweetness. It's suggested as the sweet for a weekday family dinner in a mid-1950s version of "Doctors' Orders," a pamphlet produced by the British Medical Association. The booklet also advises on ideal bedtime for children, the importance of fresh air and exercise ("husband" should start the day with a dozen knee bends and press-ups [push-ups] but nothing too violent, while wives can walk to the shops), and how to avoid constipation.

SERVES 6

To make the custard, butter an oval baking dish measuring about 10×7 inches (25×18 cm).

In a small saucepan, combine the milk and lemon zest, and bring just to a simmer over medium heat. Remove from the heat and leave to infuse for 10 minutes. Then add the butter, which will melt in the residual warmth, and stir to mix.

In a bowl, whisk together the egg yolks and sugar until the mixture is light in color, then whisk in the hot milk mixture, followed by the bread crumbs. Pour the mixture into the prepared baking dish and let stand for 30 minutes. Meanwhile, preheat the oven to 325°F (165°C).

Bake the custard until it is set, 20–25 minutes. Remove from the oven and let cool slightly. (You can do this stage in advance, letting the custard cool and then chilling it until needed. It will keep for up to 2 days.) Turn down the oven temperature to 275°F (135°C). Warm the jam slightly on the stove top or in a microwave and spread it over the top in a thin layer.

To make the meringue, in a bowl, whisk together the egg whites and cream of tartar until soft peaks form. Gradually add the sugar while whisking constantly until stiff, shiny peaks form. Pour the meringue onto the pudding, covering it completely, and, using a fork, make spiky patterns in the top. Bake until the meringue is hard to the touch and browning on top, about 20 minutes. The bottom should still be quite squidgy while the top is cooked through. Serve hot, warm, or at room temperature.

FOR THE CUSTARD

1 tablespoon butter, plus more for the baking dish

1¼ cups (300 ml) milk

Finely grated zest of 1 lemon

2 eggs yolks

2 tablespoons superfine sugar

⅔ cup (30 g) fresh bread crumbs

⅓ cup (100 g) strawberry or raspberry jam

FOR THE MERINGUE

2 egg whites

¼ teaspoon cream of tartar

½ cup (100 g) superfine sugar

SISTER EVANGELINA

(TO SISTER MONICA JOAN)

You're like a moth to a flame with meringue. You needn't think we've forgotten the Queen of Puddings!

SEASON 3: EPISODE 5

BAKEWELL TART

Bakewell tarts appear several times in Call the Midwife, *both in their individual form and as a large, open tart. Most notably, a huge Bakewell tart is on the table at a particularly fraught evening meal during Sister Ursula's brief stint in charge of Nonnatus House in season 6. Barbara is late, and Sister Monica Joan is missing, having sneaked off to watch the television Sister Ursula sent to the Poplar Seaman's Mission from a bench outside the mission's bar. The original Bakewell pudding was a deep tart or flan with custard layered over preserves or candied fruit. It wasn't invented in Bakewell—there were lots of versions of it with lots of different names—but it became associated with the Derbyshire town, a popular tourist destination, around the 1820s. However, it doesn't transport well, and by the late nineteenth century, a new version, with frangipane layered over jam, was in the ascendant. By the 1960s, it was sometimes iced and topped with a cherry, but it was also served covered with marble icing, decorated with sliced almonds, or finished with a pastry lattice top.*

SERVES 8

To make the pastry, put the flour and sugar into a bowl and stir well. Scatter the butter over the flour mixture and, using a pastry blender or your fingertips, work in the butter until it is in pieces the size of small peas. Drizzle the egg and 1 tablespoon of the water over the flour mixture and, using as few strokes as possible, stir and toss until the dough comes together in a rough mass, adding a little more water if needed to bring the pastry together. (This is easiest done in a food processor, first pulsing the butter into the flour-sugar mixture and then pulsing in the egg and water.) Do not overwork. Gently shape the dough into a thick disk in the bowl, then cover the bowl with a plate and refrigerate the dough for 30 minutes.

Butter a 9-inch (23-cm) tart pan with a removable bottom. On a lightly floured work surface, roll out the pastry into a round about 12 inches (30 cm) in diameter and ¼ inch (6 mm) thick. Line the prepared pan with the pastry, allowing the excess to drape over the sides. Using a small knife, trim the edges, leaving a ½-inch (12-mm) overhang, then roll the overhang back over itself and press against the sides of the pan. Line the pastry-lined pan with aluminum foil or parchment paper and fill with dried beans or pie weights. Chill for another 30 minutes. Preheat the oven to 350°F (180°C).

Bake the pastry for 15 minutes. Carefully remove the beans and foil, and continue to bake until the pastry is pale golden and fully cooked, about 10 minutes longer. Let cool on a wire rack.

Meanwhile, make the filling. In a bowl, using an electric mixer, beat together the butter and sugar on medium speed until the mixture is light in color and fluffy. Add the eggs, one at a time, beating well after each addition. Add the ground almonds, flour, milk, and almond extract, and beat until well mixed.

FOR THE PASTRY

1⅓ cups (170 g) flour, plus more for the work surface

¼ cup (50 g) superfine sugar

½ cup (115 g) cold butter, cut into small cubes, plus more for the pan

1 egg, lightly beaten

1–2 tablespoons ice-cold water

FOR THE FILLING

½ cup (115 g) butter, at room temperature

½ cup plus 1 tablespoon (115 g) superfine sugar

2 eggs

¾ cup plus 2 teaspoons (85 g) ground almonds

2 tablespoons flour

2½ tablespoons milk

Few drops of pure almond extract

⅓ cup (100 g) raspberry jam or jelly

Spread the bottom of the tart pastry with the raspberry jam. Add the filling, spreading it evenly. If you are decorating your tart with just sliced almonds, sprinkle them over the top now so they will toast in the oven.

Bake the tart until the filling is browned and springs back when lightly pressed with a fingertip, 20–25 minutes. Let cool completely on a wire rack. Carefully unmold the tart from the tart pan, first removing the outer ring and then gently sliding the tart off the pan bottom onto a serving plate.

If you prefer to decorate the tart with a layer of glacé icing, sift the confectioners' sugar into a bowl and then stir in the lemon juice and enough warm water to make a thick but pourable icing. Pour the icing evenly over the top of the cooled and unmolded tart and decorate with the slivered almonds and, for maximum late-1960s effect, one or more glacé cherries, if desired. Watch out though: too many and you risk hitting the 1970s. Let the icing set for about 30 minutes, then carefully unmold the tart and transfer to a serving plate.

TO DECORATE WITH ALMONDS

Small handful of sliced almonds

TO DECORATE WITH GLACÉ ICING

1 cup (115 g) confectioners' sugar

1 teaspoon fresh lemon juice

1–2 tablespoons warm water

Small handful of slivered blanched almonds

Glacé cherries (optional)

NURSE CRANE

I must say, it's most unlike Sister Monica Joan to miss an opportunity for Bakewell tart.

SEASON 6: EPISODE 3

MACARONI PUDDING

A homage to the milkman, one of the constants in Call the Midwife, *this classic milk pudding would have been familiar to the characters of the series but is almost completely forgotten now. Starchy milk puddings had their heyday in the interwar years, when many of the* Call the Midwife *characters were growing up. They remained firm favorites well into the 1960s, by now readily available canned. We see many characters enjoying rice pudding, including Reggie, for it is one of his favorite dishes. But rice wasn't the only starch to form the basis of a milk pudding. Tapioca and sago were also popular, as was semolina. This pudding uses macaroni, which, like its savory cousin, mac and cheese, crisps nicely on top while remaining satisfyingly soft underneath. It is very simple to make and ideal for all of those cast-iron ranges that still lurk in many of the dilapidated apartments seen on-screen and still very much a part of life for the poorer residents of 1950s Poplar.*

SERVES 6

Bring a saucepan filled with lightly salted water to a boil over high heat, add the macaroni, and boil for 20 minutes. Drain and return the macaroni to the pan. Add the milk and bring back to a boil over medium-high heat. Reduce the heat to a simmer and simmer until the macaroni is very tender, about 15 minutes. Remove from the heat and let cool until lukewarm.

Preheat the oven to 350°F (180°C). Butter an 8-inch (20-cm) square baking dish. Stir the sugar and egg into the cooled macaroni mixture, mixing well. Pour the macaroni mixture into the prepared dish.

Bake the pudding until the top is golden brown, about 45 minutes. Serve hot, topping each serving with a dollop of jam and with complementary berries, if desired.

½ cup (55 g) elbow macaroni

2½ cups (600 ml) milk

butter for the pan

¼ cup (50 g) sugar

1 egg, lightly beaten

Jam or marmalade of choice, for serving

Strawberries or other berries, for serving (optional)

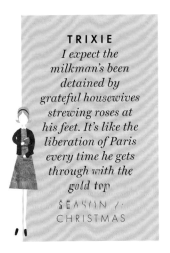

TRIXIE
I expect the milkman's been detained by grateful housewives strewing roses at his feet. It's like the liberation of Paris every time he gets through with the gold top

SEASON 7 CHRISTMAS

CHOCOLATE BLANCMANGE

Another easily made, cheap recipe based on milk with minimal extras, blancmange started life in the fourteenth century, when it was usually based on rice, almonds, and often included milk and chicken (it was just rice and almond milk on fast days). Over time, the name and contents changed, but it always stayed true to its name, which literally translates as "white eat." By the eighteenth century, it was an almond pudding or jelly (gelatin) set with isinglass (a fish-based setting agent), and in the Victorian era, it became a simple milk pudding using arrowroot or cornflour. This recipe is an early twentieth century one publicized by Brown & Polson, who made cornflour (cornstarch) and other cooking shortcuts. It was just a short step from there to ready-made mixtures, and by the 1960s, the same company was promoting its "variety custard" range in "fresh and fruity flavours." The days of blancmange were numbered. You can leave the chocolate and spice out if you want to make a plain white mixture.

SERVES 6–8

In a small bowl, whisk together 1 cup (240 ml) of the milk, the cornstarch, sugar, and salt until the dry ingredients are dissolved. In another small bowl, whisk together 1 cup (240 ml) of the milk and the cocoa powder until the cocoa powder dissolves.

Pour the remaining 3 cups (700 ml) milk into a saucepan and heat to a gentle simmer over medium-low heat. Do not allow to boil. Whisk the milk-cornstarch mixture and then the milk-cocoa mixture into the hot milk along with the vanilla extract and mixed spice (if using) and cook, whisking almost constantly and not allowing the mixture to boil, until the raw cornstarch flavor disappears and the mixture thickens, about 15 minutes.

Remove from the heat, cover with parchment paper, pressing it directly onto the surface to stop a skin from forming (or simply whisk every 5 minutes or so), and let cool for 20 minutes.

Have ready a 5-cup (1.2-l) mold (a bunny-shape mold is the absolute ideal here). When the mixture has cooled for 20 minutes, pour it into the mold. Cover and chill until set, at least 4 hours or up to 1 day. When ready to serve, simply turn out the blancmange onto a serving plate and bear, triumphantly, to table.

RECIPE NOTE For a more festive dessert, have ready lightly sweetened whipped cream in a piping bag fitted with a star tip. Then unmold the blancmange, pipe a mound of rosettes decoratively onto the center, and dust with mixed spice.

5 cups (1.2 l) milk

⅔ cup (85 g) cornstarch

⅔ cup (125 g) sugar

¼ teaspoon salt

¼ cup (20 g) unsweetened cocoa powder

1 teaspoon pure vanilla extract

1 teaspoon mixed spice (optional)

SHELAGH
You can pass me things down off the high shelves. Starting with the bunny blancmange mould, and the piping nozzles. Then go and change your tie before you head back to the surgery.

SEASON 7: EPISODE 8

FLUFFY RUFFLE

Jellies (gelatin-based desserts) and blancmanges were part of most childhoods in the 1950s and 1960s, having slowly descended from food for the upper classes in the seventeenth century to food for the nursery four hundred years later. Ready-made jelly, which came in cubes and just needed hot water added, was introduced in the 1920s, a build on earlier flavored powdered gelatin mixtures (which included the American Jell-O). It was ideal as a base for adding other ingredients, and when Carnation, the leading brand of evaporated milk, printed a recipe for jelly mixed with evaporated milk, it proved the ideal quick dessert. It was usually known as jelly fluff, but writer Heidi Thomas knew it as fluffy ruffle, which is even better. You can mix in the evaporated milk unwhipped and put the mixture in a mold, or you can whip the milk, whisk it into the cooled jelly, and serve it in a bowl as here. The result is not unlike Instant Whip or Angel Delight, fluffy packet desserts that were introduced in 1955 and 1967, respectively. Of course, you can also just eat tinned fruit with evaporated milk without doing anything fancier—very much a staple of the series.

SERVES 8

If you have space, put a bowl and the beaters for your electric mixer in the freezer for whipping the milk. Make the jelly or Jell-O according to the package instructions and let cool to room temperature. The gelatin should be viscous rather than set.

In the well-chilled bowl, using the electric mixer, whip together the evaporated milk and lemon juice on high speed until the milk triples in size and is stiff. Whisk the milk into the cooled gelatin, then transfer the mixture to a glass serving bowl. Cover and refrigerate for at least 2 hours to set fully

Just before serving, decorate with glacé cherries, candied angelica, and chocolate buttons (if using) or with berries and hundreds and thousands.

1 packet (4¾ oz/135g) jelly cubes, such as Hartley's brand, or 1 box (6 oz/170 g) Jell-O, in flavor of choice

¾ cup (180 ml) evaporated milk, well chilled

2 teaspoons fresh lemon juice

Glacé cherries, candied angelica, and chocolate buttons (optional) or fresh berries of choice and hundreds and thousands, for decorating

DR TURNER
I've just found a blackcurrant jelly and a tin of evap on the step.

TIMOTHY
Another kindly patient must've put them there after Mrs. Penny left.

SEASON 6:
EPISODE 4

BEHIND THE SCENES

The leafy lanes of Surrey are a long way from the grime and bustle of the East End of London, but it's off a nondescript road in the stockbroker belt where you'll find the *Call the Midwife* set. At its heart is a rambling Victorian manor house taken over by the Ministry of Defence in the 1950s and used as an officers' mess for many years. Now its elegant Edwardian fittings and molded ceilings form a backdrop to the temporary walls and renovated midcentury furniture of the fictional Nonnatus House.

Walk up the stairs and through the distinctive door and step back into the 1960s. The house is ideal: The existing nineteenth and twentieth century décor is exactly what you'd expect from a slightly tired building repurposed as a nunnery in a rapidly changing urban landscape. The rooms are big enough (mainly) to hold all the cast and crew necessary to bring the show to our screens, which, in the case of the birth scenes, includes midwives and mothers as well as technicians, directors, and actors.

Prior to each season, a huge team of set builders and art crew descends on the site, repairing the fiberglass walls that make the railway arch and its surrounds, building interiors on a sound stage to one side, and ensuring that all the doors on the replica streets that lead away from the main set open onto appropriately decorated walls, even if they then stop abruptly in a garden. Nonnatus House occupies just the central block of the original manor. Open the wrong door and you'll find yourself in the maternity hospital, or Matthew's flat, or Miss Higgins' sitting room. All of these have permanent features—the shelving, the exquisite curved kitchen of Nonnatus House, the dining table, and the fireplaces—but there's also a props team waiting in the wings with a store full of movable objects to bring it all to life.

The attention to detail is easy to miss when you're glued to the television. But pause and look at the shelves behind Fred in his newsagent, or peek into the cupboards at the Turners' house. You'll see period packaging, researched and replicated by the art department, made up into cereal boxes or glued round tins. The serried ranks of chocolate bars on display in the shop are actually wood, and some of the scones in the café are plastic, but most of the food is made to order and, if not actually edible by the time it's been adjusted to stand the heat and light of filming, was once a real recipe.

Many of the *Call the Midwife* viewers will remember the 1960s, and, of course, a lot of the things in use then were still in everyday use decades later. Thus, we see Royal Doulton Reflection ware on the Nonnatus table, along with Wood's Beryl designs,

> ### NURSE CRANE
> *It was the Big Top I was admiring, not the snow. And I'd be obliged if you didn't tell me how you make the magic. It might interfere with my imaginative process.*
>
> SEASON 10: CHRISTMAS

which were ubiquitous in institutional contexts, such as the Iris Knight Institute in the show, until at least the 1990s. The props store holds shelves of dining ware suitable for any occasion, be it tea in the West End or abject poverty in the East. The amber-color Sowerby glassware is pure 1930s but would not look out of place today. Upstairs in the store are the larger items: a corridor of larder units, a line of unfitted kitchens, and a row of ovens in various states of disrepair. When a room is ready to be dressed, the various props, small and large, will be spruced up and put together into collections ready to go on set, ensuring that things aren't repeated across rooms, for eagle-eyed viewers will write in and comment.

Of course, the Surrey set isn't the only place to experience the *Call the Midwife* magic. And it's not open to the public. But you can visit Chatham docks, where many of the exteriors (and some interiors) are filmed, including what's become known as "washing line alley." The East End itself also provides some of the exterior views—a block of flats here, a church there—but much of it is very different now. What you see on-screen is a true patchwork: objects bought or found, sets built to order and that last only a few weeks, and rooms that have barely changed since the early 1900s. It's a testament to all the unseen—but vital—behind-the-scenes crew that we never notice the joins but only wonder instead just where we can buy such brilliant plates for our own *Call the Midwife*–themed dinner parties.

BANANA FLOWERPOTS

Banana with custard was the go-to sweet, snack, and comfort food for Britain for at least a generation after the war (some people added cornflakes as well, including my grandfather, who ate this mixture every night for about fifty years). In episode 6, season 7, it's what Trixie reaches for in the aftermath of her breakup with Christopher Dockerill: simple, warming, and, if you use custard powder, ready within minutes. This recipe, a riff on one in Elizabeth Craig's 1962 book, Banana Dishes, *is a build on the basic principle and a dish guaranteed to raise a wry smile. The book itself is a delight and includes a number of eyebrow-raising recipes, such as banana and sausage rolls, banana flambé, and banana and onion soup. Some, clearly, should really use plantain, which was virtually unknown in Britain in the 1960s. Others are simply a reminder that bananas were still somewhat exotic. Craig's hula-hula soup used them mixed with canned green pea soup, canned turtle soup, sherry, and whipped cream—not one for the average docker's family in Poplar. I have included directions for homemade custard here, but if you're rushed for time, custard powder (see 1960s Spin) or tinned custard is fine.*

SERVES 4

To make the custard, in a saucepan, whisk together the milk, egg yolks, sugar, and cornstarch until the cornstarch is fully dissolved. Place over medium-high heat and bring to a gentle boil, whisking continuously. Reduce the heat to medium and simmer, whisking often, until thickened, 2–3 minutes. Remove from the heat and stir in the vanilla to taste. Cover with a round of parchment paper pressed directly onto the surface to stop a skin from forming and set aside until cool. You should have 2 cups (480 ml).

In a bowl, mash the bananas with a fork, then distribute evenly among four 1-cup (240-ml) cups. Pour the custard on top, dividing it evenly. Sprinkle with the grated chocolate (to look like soil), decorate with the flowers, and serve.

 1960s SPIN *Although you can make your own custard, you really don't have to. Custard powder was used by nearly everyone in the 1950s and 1960s. The main brand was Bird's, made in Birmingham and invented by Alfred Bird, who also pioneered baking powder in Britain. He invented custard powder because his wife Elizabeth couldn't eat eggs. It's essentially cornstarch, vanilla flavoring, and yellow coloring, which you mix with milk and sugar to taste. It remains a British staple.*

FOR THE CUSTARD

2 cups (500 ml) milk

3 egg yolks

¼ cup (50 g) sugar

2 heaped tablespoons cornstarch

1–2 teaspoons pure vanilla extract

FOR SERVING

4 ripe bananas, peeled

6 oz (170 g) dark chocolate, grated

Edible fresh flowers, such as viola, pansy, nasturtium, cornflower, or dandelion, on their stalks, or crystallized flowers in winter, for decorating

TRIXIE
A pan of custard is hardly a nutritional crime. Besides, I'm going to pour it over this sliced banana, so vitamin C will be involved.

SEASON 6:
EPISODE 7

APPLE STRUDEL

Apple strudels feature in a couple of Call the Midwife *episodes, both revolving around the tribulations of Eastern European Jewish families. On each occasion we're reminded that the horrors of the Holocaust and the Second World War were only a decade or so distant at the time the series is set, and that the effects were lifelong. The East End was home to a large population of Jewish immigrants who had fled persecution in Eastern Europe and settled to new lives in London. As with the other immigrant families we meet in* Call the Midwife, *they brought with them traditions from their homelands, including culinary ones. Many of them would eventually filter through to the mainstream, enriching the culture of their new homes.*

Strudels originated in Eastern Europe, though exactly where is disputed, and many countries lay claim to them. By the eighteenth century, they were particularly associated with Austria and later became an intrinsic part of Viennese café culture. They're name-checked in "My Favorite Things," one of the most memorable songs in The Sound of Music, *which the nuns go and see in season 9, after much lobbying from Sister Monica Joan. The Apfelstrudel was the most recognizable type, though there were many other fillings, both sweet and savory.* Strudel *means "whirlpool" in German, and the crisp, wrapped pastry should form delicate layers. The pastry is best when made at home, and recipes from the time give lengthy instructions. However, in the twenty-first century, you can cheat and use filo.*

SERVES 6–8

Preheat the oven to 400°F (200°C). Line a sheet pan with parchment paper or a silicone baking mat and brush lightly with a little of the butter.

In a large bowl, combine the apples, currants, brown sugar, almonds, bread crumbs, cinnamon, allspice, and citrus zests, and toss and stir together until evenly mixed.

Unroll the filo sheets on a dry work surface and cover with a kitchen towel to prevent them from drying out. Lay one filo sheet on the prepared pan and brush with some of the butter. Top with a second sheet and brush with more butter. Repeat until all the filo sheets are stacked, reserving 1–2 tablespoons butter for brushing on top once the strudel is rolled.

Spread the filling in a heap lengthwise along the center of the filo stack, leaving about 1¼ inches (3 cm) uncovered at each short end and about 2½ inches (6 cm) uncovered on each long side. Now, working from a long side, fold the pastry around the filling, using the parchment or baking mat to help lift it, then fold in the short sides and gently roll up, finishing seam side down. Brush the pastry with the remaining butter.

Bake the strudel until the pastry is golden brown and the filling is cooked, 40–50 minutes. It can be served hot, warm, or at room temperature. Dust with the confectioners' sugar immediately before serving.

½ cup (115 g) butter, melted and cooled

½ lb (225 g) Bramley or other cooking apples, peeled, cored, and thinly sliced

½ lb (225 g) Cox's Orange Pippin, Braeburn, or other eating apples, peeled, cored, and thinly sliced

2 tablespoons dried currants

⅓ cup (85 g) firmly packed light brown sugar

3 tablespoons chopped toasted almonds

1 tablespoon fine dried bread crumbs

1 teaspoon ground cinnamon

½ teaspoon ground allspice

Finely grated zest of 1 orange

Finely grated zest of 1 lemon

8 large sheets filo pastry, thawed in the refrigerator if frozen

1 tablespoon confectioners' sugar, for dusting

RHUBARB CRUMBLE

A mainstay of any allotment, we see rhubarb growing in Fred's plot, and at various times, we also see its enthusiastic consumption. In season 8, Sister Monica Joan bonds with Clarice Millgrove over raw rhubarb dipped in sugar. Clarice's storyline, as a former suffragette whose accounts of her brutal treatment as she fought for women's right to vote, acts as a counterpoint to Violet's campaign for election to the local council: a reminder of how far society had come in just one lifetime. Rhubarb was more usually cooked, however, including in tarts, jams, puddings, and, perhaps one of the most quintessentially British dishes, crumble. Contrary to its reputation as a traditional British pudding, crumble actually dates to the Second World War, when its (then) sparse topping was a way of giving a pastry-like lift to fruit puddings, using whatever fat was around and only limited flour and sugar. Custard is pretty much the obligatory accompaniment for this crumble, and directions for it are included here. Or you can reach for the tub of custard powder if you are short of time.

SERVES 4–6

Preheat the oven to 400°F (200°C). Butter a 9-inch (23-cm) baking dish.

To make the filling, spread the rhubarb evenly in the prepared dish. Sprinkle the granulated sugar and orange juice evenly over the rhubarb.

To make the topping, put the flour into a bowl and scatter the butter over the top. Using a pastry blender or your fingertips, work the butter into the flour just until the mixture is the consistency of bread crumbs. (You can do this in a food processor using the pulse function; be careful not to overwork it.) Stir in the Demerara sugar and orange zest. Your crumble topping should look like bread crumbs and definitely not like pastry. Sprinkle the mixture over the rhubarb and level off the top.

Bake the crumble until the top is crispy and the filling is just bubbling through, 35–40 minutes.

Toward the end of baking, begin making the custard. In a small bowl, whisk together 2 tablespoons of the milk and the cornstarch until the cornstarch dissolves, then set aside. Pour the remaining milk into a saucepan and heat over medium heat to just below the boiling point, then remove from the heat. While the milk heats, in a bowl, whisk the egg yolks until blended, then whisk in the sugar. Slowly pour the hot milk into the egg yolk mixture while whisking continuously until the sugar dissolves. Now pour the egg yolk–milk mixture back into the pan, then whisk the cornstarch mixture just to recombine and whisk into the milk mixture, mixing well. Place over medium-high heat and bring to a gentle boil, whisking continuously. Reduce the heat to medium and simmer, whisking often, until thickened, 2–3 minutes. Remove from the heat and stir in the vanilla to taste.

Butter, for the baking dish

FOR THE FILLING

1⅔ lb (750 g) rhubarb, trimmed and sliced ¼ inch (6 mm) thick

⅓ cup plus 1½ tablespoons (85 g) granulated sugar

Juice of 1 orange

FOR THE TOPPING

⅔ cup (85 g) flour

6 tablespoons (90 g) cold butter, cut into small cubes

¼ cup (50 g) Demerara sugar

Finely grated zest of 1 orange

FOR THE CUSTARD

2 cups (480 ml) milk

2 heaped tablespoons cornstarch

3 egg yolks

¼ cup (50 g) granulated sugar

1–2 tablespoons pure vanilla extract

Recipe continues on the following page

Continued from the previous page

Serve the crumble hot with the hot custard in a jug on the side. You can also serve the crumble cold with hot custard, but it isn't as nice.

RECIPE NOTE You can use any fruit for the filling. Apples are widely used, but plums, quinces, fresh red and black currants, gooseberries, pears, and just about anything else you can think of will work. Just adjust the sugar to suit the fruit. If you are using a tougher fruit, such as quinces or some cooking pears, precook the filling. You can also add a spice or two. Some recipes use rolled oats in place of some of the flour, and others run some ground nuts through the topping as well. It's entirely up to you.

LUCILLE
Miss Millgrove?
May I come in?
I brought you a
present. Rhubarb
with sugar, and a
little bit of salt.

SEASON 8:
EPISODE 2

FRUIT FOOL

Tinned fruit with evaporated milk is the standard pudding for many of the Call the Midwife *households, and it was an absolute classic of the time. However, a proper fruit fool isn't a million miles away, is equally of the era, and is more geared toward modern palates (though you can, of course, just mix tinned fruit and evaporated milk and feel thoroughly of the time).*

Fools have a very long history, going right back to the Tudor era (and conceptually even further). Early fools were custard-based and frequently flavored with rose water or sweet spices. By the 1950s, they were generally very plain, but are none the worse for that. You can use any fruit you have, but given there are only three ingredients, it's worth sourcing good-quality fruit at its peak. That said, a canned purée would have been the Poplar solution in most cases. Sharp fruits, such as rhubarb, gooseberries, and red currants, work particularly well, but pears, plums, strawberries, and other soft fruits are also excellent.

SERVES 4

Prepare the fruit for cooking by peeling and coring such fruits as pears or apples and stemming such fruits as currants or gooseberries. Chop larger fruits into small, uniform chunks. If you are using a soft fruit, such as strawberries or raspberries, there is no need to cook it, and you can skip the next stage. If you are using rhubarb, gooseberries, pears, or apples, put the pieces into a pan and add the water and the sugar according to the tartness of the fruit. Place over medium heat, stir well, and cook, stirring often and adjusting the heat as needed to prevent scorching, until tender. The timing will depend on the fruit.

Whether you've used cooked or uncooked fruit, purée it with an immersion or stand blender until very smooth and fairly thick, adding sugar to taste to the uncooked fruit as you purée. Transfer to a bowl, cover, and refrigerate until well chilled.

Just before serving, in a bowl, using a whisk or an electric mixer on medium-high speed, whip the cream until stiff peaks form. Then simply fold the whipped cream into the chilled fruit purée. It is up to you whether you fold it in until no white streaks remain or go for a marbled effect. Serve the fool in a large glass bowl or in individual glasses.

1 lb (450 g) fruit of choice (see headnote)

¼ cup (60 ml) water

4–5 tablespoons (50–75 g) sugar

1¼ cups (300 ml) heavy cream

MRS. LECK
Sister! Ah, I heard you was poorly! Oh, am I glad to see you out and about again. Can I tempt you to a bit of fruit today? On the house, you take your pick.

SISTER MONICA JOAN
How very kind! I will not suffer my pale forehead to be kissed by nightshade, or the ruby grape of Proserpine. I'll have a pound of those pears.

SEASON 1: EPISODE 6

ORANGE ORGIES

Sometimes the glory of the 1950s is its sheer exuberance. Postwar, there was a real feeling of making up for lost time. For those who kept up with the trends, food was bigger, brighter, and just more sheer fun than ever before. The word orgy *didn't have quite the meaning it does today—or rather, the sexual element was just one part of the meaning. Orgy was generally taken to mean an excess, especially in a party context. It also carried a whiff of the religious ceremony about it. So while the name of this recipe would certainly have raised an eyebrow, it wouldn't have been quite as risqué as it seems now. It appeared in a pamphlet published by* Weekend Magazine, *a rival to* Tit-Bits, *a name we sometimes hear in* Call the Midwife, *not usually in an approving context. Buckle's newsagent certainly would have stocked it.*

SERVES 4

Using a sharp knife, cut the top one-third off of each orange, stopping just short of cutting all the way through to create a "hinged" lid. Using a grapefruit spoon or other sharp-edge spoon, carefully separate the flesh of the orange from the peel, scooping it out onto a cutting board. Trim off and discard all the pith and membrane from the flesh and dice the flesh into small pieces. Transfer the diced orange to a bowl and sprinkle with the orange-flower water, if using.

Peel the banana and cut into small dice. Add it to the orange pieces along with the dates and nuts, and mix gently. Spoon this mixture into the orange cases, filling them to just below the rim. In a small bowl, whisk the cream until soft peaks form, then spoon (or pipe) the cream onto the filling. Gently lower the lid on each orange so it sits on the cream.

Serve the orgies immediately. The original serving suggestion is to use a lettuce leaf as a bed on which to sit each orgy, but this may be a stretch too weird for modern tastes.

RECIPE NOTE If the idea of a hinged lid doesn't appeal, you can also present these oranges as baskets. Either remove the lid completely and use a strip of candied angelica or candied or plain orange peel to form a handle over the cream, or cut the top off in such a way as to leave a strip of orange peel intact, which is fiddly but impressive. You can apply the same basic presentation idea to all sorts of other fruits, including apples and pineapples, filling them with sweet mixtures as here or with salad.

4 oranges

½ teaspoon orange-flower water or triple sec (optional)

1 banana

½ cup (70 g) chopped dates

½ cup (70 g) chopped nuts (cashews or hazelnuts work best)

½ cup (120 ml) heavy cream

Lettuce, for serving (optional)

TRIXIE
When Christian Dior commissioned this, he said to his perfumiers, "Create a fragrance that's like love."

VALERIE
Hmm, so he got a hundred roses, a big bunch of jasmine, and squeezed them in a bottle with a dash of Lemon Pledge?

TRIXIE
Oh, Valerie! That's the heart note of chypre and Sicilian oranges!

SEASON 7: EPISODE 1

ICE CREAM SODAS

One of the simplest recipes in this book, ice cream sodas appear in the first episode of season 11. As ever, it's an emotional start to the new season, but it is also Nurse Corrigan's first day on the staff roster, and it's mid-May, so it's time for the annual joy that is the Eurovision Song Contest. Eurovision has since grown to huge proportions—yet remains a glorious celebration of the eclecticism of musical taste—but in 1967, only seventeen countries participated. Vienna hosted, and the stage not only had a central stair but revolving mirrors—and the competition's first Black entrant (representing Portugal). Despite Sister Julienne's initial misgivings, everyone at Nonnatus House watches the contest together after Fred's television breaks, bopping along with foaming ice cream sodas. Such delights were, as Nurse Corrigan notes, going out of fashion by then, after booming in the interwar era and just after. They were invented in America in the 1870s, became hugely popular during Prohibition in the 1920s, and made the leap to Britain partly due to the lure of America and partly because the soda fountain and its glamourous trappings were a new and exciting way to spend time. The recognition of young adults as "teenagers" in the 1950s also helped. However, the even cooler Italian-style coffee bars rapidly eclipsed milk bars, and ice cream sodas retreated into the background.

SERVES 2

Put one scoop of ice cream in the bottom of each of two tall glasses. Top up with soda water or lemonade—the former is more refreshing and the latter is sweeter and more of a crowd-pleaser. Add the cordial and allow the whole thing to fizz up pleasingly. Include a long-handled spoon with each soda. Paper straws are optional but very helpful.

2 scoops vanilla or other ice cream of choice

2½ cups (600 ml) soda water or lemonade

2 teaspoons black currant, strawberry, or other cordial of choice

 1960s SPIN *To drink these in true Call the Midwife style, you need the right soundtrack. Sandie Shaw's "Puppet on a String" won the Eurovision Contest that year for Britain, which hosted the contest the following year. However, it wasn't the only massive hit to emerge from Eurovision in the 1950s and 1960s. The same year that Shaw won, Luxembourg's Vicky sang "L'amour est bleu," which was widely covered despite only coming in fourth. Luxembourg won in 1965 when France Gall sang "Poupée de cire, poupée de son." Then there's "Nel blu, dipinto di blu," Italy's winner in 1958 and etched into many a brain since. Britain won again in 1969 with Lulu and "Boom Bang-a-Bang." Honorable mention, too, for Cliff Richard, who came in second in 1968 with "Congratulations."*

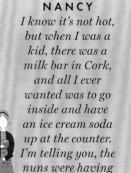

NANCY
I know it's not hot, but when I was a kid, there was a milk bar in Cork, and all I ever wanted was to go inside and have an ice cream soda up at the counter. I'm telling you, the nuns were having none of it.

SEASON 11:
EPISODE 1

BLACK FOREST GÂTEAU

Black forest cake, or gâteau as it is usually known in Britain, was the quintessential restaurant dessert of the 1970s, but it was creeping into popular consciousness at the end of the 1960s. Its exact origins are murky. Various people claim to have written down the first recipe at several points in the 1930s, but it didn't appear in print until the 1960s. The flavor combination was mentioned in a German context in the early nineteenth century, however, and it has definite German roots. As with a number of dishes of the 1960s, its sudden popularity seems to have come from America, where recipes for it were circulating by the early 1960s. It was loved by restaurant chefs, as it was relatively easy to prepare in advance, looked stupendous—especially as the number of layers started to climb in the 1970s—and was a crowd-pleaser in terms of taste. This version is a low-key one and uses cherries steeped in brandy, the original form of the maraschino cherries so loved by the Call the Midwife *nurses in the cocktail sessions of seasons 1 through 5.*

SERVES 8–10

To make the sponge, preheat the oven to 350°F (180°C). Butter the bottom and sides of two 8-inch (20-cm) round cake pans. Line the bottoms with parchment paper and coat the sides lightly with a mix of equal parts flour and sugar, tapping out the excess.

In a stand mixer fitted with the whip attachment, or in a large bowl with a handheld mixer, beat the egg whites on medium-high speed until stiff peaks form. Add the sugar in three batches alternately with the egg yolks in three batches, beating well after each addition and adding the salt with the last batch of sugar. Once all the sugar and egg yolks are incorporated, continue to beat on medium-high speed until the mixture is thick and creamy, about 10 minutes.

In a small bowl, stir together the cocoa powder, milk, and vanilla until the cocoa dissolves. In a medium bowl, sift together the flour and baking powder. Fold the flour mixture into the egg mixture in three batches alternately with the cocoa mixture in two batches, beginning and ending with the flour mixture and making sure no white streaks remain after the final addition. Divide the batter evenly between the prepared pans.

Bake the cake layers until a skewer inserted into the center comes out clean, 20–25 minutes. Let cool in the pans on wire racks for 10 minutes, then invert onto the racks, lift off the pans, peel off the parchment, turn upright, and let cool completely.

FOR THE CHOCOLATE SPONGE

Butter, for the pans

2/3 cup (85 g) flour, plus more for the pans

1 cup plus 2 tablespoons (225 g) superfine sugar, plus more for the pans

3 eggs, separated

Pinch of salt

3 tablespoons unsweetened cocoa powder

2 tablespoons milk

1/2 teaspoon pure vanilla extract

1/2 teaspoon baking powder

FOR THE GANACHE

4 oz (115 g) dark chocolate, roughly chopped

3/4 cup (180 ml) heavy cream

TO ASSEMBLE

2 1/2 cups (600 ml) heavy cream

Generous amount of cherries in brandy, for filling and decorating

Dark chocolate, grated, for decorating

Recipe continues on the following page

Continued from the previous page

To make the ganache, put the chocolate into a small heatproof bowl. In a small saucepan, heat the cream over medium heat to just below the boiling point. Pour the hot cream over the chocolate, let stand for 4–5 minutes to melt, and then stir vigorously until the ganache is thick and shiny. Do not overwork. Let cool completely. Just before using, whisk until light and fluffy.

When you are ready to assemble the cake, begin by whipping the cream to soft peaks. If the cherries aren't pitted, do it now.

Put the less aesthetically pleasing cake layer on a serving plate and brush it with a good helping of brandy from the cherries (about 3 tablespoons). Using a palette knife or an offset spatula, spread a thin layer of the chocolate ganache over the cake layer. Top the ganache with some cherries, arranging them in a single layer and pressing them lightly into the ganache to hold them in place. Spoon just enough of the cream over the berries to cover them (not too much or it will ooze out), smoothing it with the palette knife. Cover the top of the second cake layer with the remaining ganache and then pop it on top of the first layer.

Use one-third of the remaining cream to cover the sides of the cake, applying it smoothly with the palette knife. Spoon the remaining cream into a piping bag fitted with a small plain tip and pipe it onto the top of the cake, either in blobs or concentric circles. Decorate between the blobs or circles with more cherries (don't be mean with them). Alternatively, fit the piping bag with a large closed star tip, pipe a wide, attractive border around the top of the cake, and decorate the border with cherries. Finally, decorate the sides of the cake with the grated chocolate. Chill until serving.

1960s SPIN *There's no definitive black forest cake recipe, so you can riff freely. In television chef Delia Smith's first book,* How to Cheat at Cooking, *published in 1971, she suggests using a frozen chocolate fresh cream sponge, canned cherries drained and steeped in brandy, instant chocolate sauce, and whipped cream. The assembly takes place while the sponge is still partially frozen and the whole thing is then left in the fridge to defrost ready for service. Other recipes cook down the syrup from canned cherries to use as a sauce and brush the sponges with kirsch. You can also decorate the top of the cake with glacé cherries, rather than brandied cherries.*

KNICKERBOCKER GLORY

Although it has American roots, the Knickerbocker glory is a peculiarly British phenomenon that peaked in the 1960s and 1970s. It's a variation of the ice cream sundae, always served in a tall, very thick glass (to make it look more generous) and with a long-handled spoon. The name Knickerbocker originates with Washington Irving, who used it to denote New Yorkers of Dutch descent, and although it was also a genuine name, it was Irving who made it famous. By the end of the nineteenth century, New York had a Knickerbocker Hotel, there was a Knickerbocker Ice Company, and knickerbockers was the name for baggy-kneed, cropped trousers. In Britain, knickerbockers was also used for girls' underwear in the same style and, eventually, became the generally used term for, well, knickers (panties in the United States). The connection with the dessert is less obvious, though various stories have been suggested. The most plausible explanation is that the Lyons chain of tearooms came up with it in the 1920s (it had other garment-themed dishes), and that it caught the imagination of the British because of the very mild whiff of seaside smut in the name. It was generally a catering dish, easily made to order from tinned fruit, ready-made sauce, and, in time, aerosol whipped cream, and is one of those dishes that can be as upmarket or as cheap and cheery as you like. However, it's mainly about looks, not taste, so this version is on the easy end of the scale.

SERVES 2

Prepare two Knickerbocker glory glasses by slipping them into the freezer to chill (you can also use tall, thick highball-style glasses). Get the ice cream out to soften slightly. In a bowl, whisk the cream until soft peaks form (or reach for an aerosol can—nobody will judge).

Remove the glasses from the freezer. Put a glacé cherry in the bottom of each glass. Top each cherry with a scoop of ice cream and spoon 1 tablespoon of the sauce over the ice cream. Now add one-fourth of the fruit cocktail to each glass and then another scoop of ice cream. Add another 1 tablespoon sauce to each glass and then the rest of the fruit. If you think you can cope, add another scoop of ice cream to each glass. Add the rest of the sauce, dividing it between the glasses.

Top each sundae with a generous amount of cream, making sure it is well above the level of the glass. Sprinkle liberally with hundreds and thousands (if using), pop a cherry on the top, and plunge a wafer or waferlike thing into the cream. Serve immediately, with a long spoon.

RECIPE NOTE You can, obviously, use fresh fruit, but stick to stuff with a bit of pizzazz, such as pineapple, mango, banana, grapes, or the like. The sauce in a Knickerbocker glory was always red, so a homemade raspberry or strawberry purée or an upmarket ready-made cherry sauce would work well. And yes, you can add a slug of cherry brandy. You can also vary the ice cream, but with all the other flavors going on, you'd be wise not to. If you must switch out the vanilla, strawberry works, but be warned that chocolate is too overpowering.

4–6 scoops vanilla ice cream

1 cup (240 ml) heavy cream

4 glacé or maraschino cherries

1 cup (240 ml) raspberry or cherry sauce or compote

1 small can (8½ oz/240 g) fruit cocktail

Hundreds and thousands, for sprinkling (optional)

2 ready-made wafers, amaretti biscuits, or chocolate cigars

TRIXIE
I think I need someone to go help me choose a different one. Perhaps we could and look in Boots, after we've eaten our Knickerbocker Glories.

SEASON 6: EPISODE 8

PINEAPPLE PAVLOVA

The origins of the pavlova are hotly contested. It was named after the Russian ballerina, Anna Pavlova, who visited both New Zealand and Australia in 1926, and both countries claim the sweet as theirs. The name was first used in New Zealand, and the idea of a large, delightfully squidgy meringue with a topping seems to have originated there, too, but they were not, at first, used together. That honor may well be an Australian one. However the pavlova started, by the 1930s, it was established in its modern form and rapidly became one of the national dishes of both countries, exported thereafter across the globe. This version uses tinned pineapple, a very popular pantry item in 1950s Britain. Pineapple still carried a hint of luxury about it from centuries of it being unavailable to anyone except the very rich. It had been widely available canned since the expansion of James Dole's Hawaiian Pineapple Company in the 1920s and 1930s, but had, of course, virtually disappeared during rationing, so was newly luxurious again when Call the Midwife *opens in 1956.*

SERVES 4–6

Preheat the oven to 325°F (165°C). Line a sheet pan with parchment paper.

In a stand mixer fitted with the whip attachment, beat together the egg whites and salt on high speed until foamy. Gradually beat in the sugar and continue to beat until the whites hold stiff, glossy peaks. Beat in the cornstarch and vinegar.

Spoon the egg whites onto the prepared sheet pan in 6–8 dollops of equal size, spacing the mounds 1–2 inches (2.5–5 cm) apart. Use the back of the spoon to make an indentation in the center of each mound. Or, to make one large meringue, spoon the egg whites into a single large mound, then use the spoon to create a wide indentation in the center.

Bake the meringue for 2 minutes, then reduce the oven temperature to 250°F (120°C) and continue to bake until crisp to the touch, about 1 hour for individual meringues or 1 hour and 40 minutes for a large meringue. Turn off the oven and leave the meringue(s) in the oven to cool completely, about 2 hours or up to overnight.

Using the stand mixer on medium-high speed or in a bowl with a whisk, whip the cream until stiff peaks form. If the pineapple is in slices, cut it into bite-size chunks. If using the ginger, cut each piece in half or in thirds.

To serve, place the small meringues on individual plates or the large meringue on a serving plate. Fill the center(s) with the cream. Top with the pineapple chunks, almonds, and ginger (if using) and serve immediately.

3 egg whites

Pinch of salt

¾ cup plus 1½ tablespoons (170 g) superfine sugar

1 teaspoon cornstarch

½ teaspoon malt vinegar

1¼ cups (300 ml) heavy cream

1 can (8 oz/225 g) pineapple, drained

8 pieces crystallized ginger (optional)

1 tablespoon sliced almonds, toasted

MOTHER MILDRED
I think it's better not to enquire into the provenance of that pineapple.

SEASON 8: EPISODE 6

1960s SPIN *In the 1960s, pavlovas come in all sorts of shapes and sizes and with all sorts of fillings. One book (which came down firmly on the side of New Zealand as the pavlova's country of origin) suggested that pineapple and passion fruit were the favored fruits in New Zealand, along with raspberries, strawberries, lemon curd, and chocolate. Fresh and tinned fruits were used, and, inevitably, the presentation suggestions involved a lot of glacé cherries.*

CHRISTMAS

The Christmas specials for *Call the Midwife* started following the success of season 1. Each one starts in the year that the preceding season is set but takes place over both Christmas and New Year's, ending in the year of the next season. On British television, the new season has always started within a few weeks of the Christmas special; of late, it's followed on directly. For that reason, the very first Christmas special technically falls within season 2. That leads to some confusion, but here the number of each episode follows that of the scripts, and therefore you won't find a season 1 Christmas special, but you will find references to the Christmas special of season 11, which was shown on December 25, 2021.

The Christmas episodes are longer than those in the main seasons and thus allow the telling of slightly more involved stories. They also offer the opportunity to do something a little different, like go to South Africa to explore themes around the breakdown of empire and white saviorhood (season 6), or to the Outer Hebrides, where Sister Monica Joan undergoes a spiritual journey and we're reminded of the stark cultural differences that can exist even with a nominally united nation (season 9). But there's scope for truly joyful moments, too. Think of Nurse Crane on a trapeze in season 10, or of Patrick and Shelagh's wedding in season 3 (1959).

Food is integral to the British Christmas, and while Christmas dinner is rarely a focus—Fred-shaped turkey-plucking disasters aside—culinary reference points are scattered throughout the Christmas specials. There's Shelagh Turner intent upon her mince pies having a different twist every year, or her children making shortbread and gingerbread decorated to look like nurses. The Christmas pudding, without which Christmas was unthinkable in the 1950s and 1960s, flames in some episodes (and boils dry in others). We see the Nonnatus residents tuck into chicken,

---

NURSE CRANE
Go on, Millicent. If you could have anything you fancied for your Christmas dinner, what would it be?

MISS HIGGINS
I hardly dare tell you. It's almost too disgraceful.

NURSE CRANE
If I had my way, I'd have a nice plain plate of baked beans on toast and a milk stout, in a lady's glass.

MISS HIGGINS
I wouldn't have a savoury course at all. I'd go straight *to the sweet. And it would be a simply* enormous *bowl of trifle, washed down with a Harvey Wallbanger.*

NURSE CRANE
A Harvey what?

MISS HIGGINS
It's an orange-coloured cocktail that tastes somewhat of aniseed, generally embellished with a small umbrella. In 1926 I had one at a Charleston contest. It's lingered in my memory ever since.

SEASON 10: CHRISTMAS

still very expensive at the time, or capon (a castrated cockerel, a process that makes the flesh plumper and whiter but is now legal in Britain). Later, reflecting the fashion of the time, turkey becomes more common.

Although it's rarely labored, *Call the Midwife* does show changing times. Along with turkey eclipsing other meats, we also see the potato accompaniment change from boiled to roasted. It comes with sprouts as well as other vegetables. And Lucille and Cyril introduce Caribbean flavors in the form of black cake, a rich, fruity cake full of wine and rum. There are hints of change, too, in the inclusion in season 8 of a novelty cake—the marshmallow snowman—ostensibly for the children.

Christmas cake is also omnipresent (the British love of dark, fruity flavors really comes to the fore in December). There we see continuity in the habit the nuns share with many families—then and now—of using the same length of ribbon around the cake and the same plastic decorations on top. Both the cake and the pudding would almost certainly have been made according to recipes from before the war. When something is only cooked once a year, it tends to evolve very slowly.

CHRISTMAS
SPECIALS

JENNY

I live in a convent, Alec. You'll get no sympathy from me.
Are you looking forward to coming for Christmas dinner?

ALEC

Absolutely.

JENNY

The Sisters couldn't invite you fast enough when I
told them your parents live in Ceylon.

SEASON 3: CHRISTMAS

MINCE PIES

Mincemeat has its origins in the medieval period, when richly spiced pies filled with meat and dried fruit were part of celebratory fare for the rich. By the end of the sixteenth century, they were associated particularly with Christmas and were often fashioned into one big pie that made an ideal gift. Over the next three hundred years, the meat content gradually dwindled, though almost all mincemeats continued to use beef suet as a key ingredient, so they were by no means vegetarian. By the 1950s, mince pies (or mincemeat tarts, as they are also known) were eaten only around Christmas and, apart from the suet, had no meat at all.

This recipe goes even further, using butter in place of suet and no alcohol, usually a staple of mincemeats. It was written down by a hard-pressed cook during rationing, when suet, dried fruit, and sugar were in short supply. Call the Midwife *opens a mere two years after rationing ended, and markers of the deprivation of the war years are everywhere. It's a reminder that even when times were hard, delicious things were still possible. Mince pies are a particularly noticeable part of Shelagh Turner's Christmas preparations: Every year she tries something different, so feel free to experiment with pastry types, flavors, or decoration.*

MAKES 12 SMALL PIES

To make the mincemeat, in a bowl, combine the apples, dark and golden raisins, currants, candied peel, Demerara sugar, butter, lemon juice, mixed spice, and salt, and mix well. You will have more mincemeat than you need for the tarts. The remainder can be stored in a tightly capped jar or other airtight container in the refrigerator or freezer for up to 6 months.

To make the pastry, in a bowl, stir together the flour and granulated sugar. Scatter the butter over the flour mixture and, using a pastry blender, cut in the butter until the mixture resembles coarse bread crumbs. Drizzle the egg evenly over the flour mixture and, using as few strokes as possible, stir and toss with a fork, adding just enough of the water, 1 tablespoon at a time, for the dough to come together in a shaggy mass. Do not overwork. (This is easiest done in a food processor, first pulsing the butter into the flour-sugar mixture and then pulsing in the egg and water.) Gently shape the dough into a thick disk in the bowl, cover the bowl with a plate, and refrigerate the dough for 30 minutes.

Preheat the oven to 400°F (200°C). Butter a 12-cup fairy cake pan or standard muffin pan.

FOR THE MINCEMEAT

2 eating apples, peeled, cored, and grated on the large holes of a box grater

1/3 cup (55 g) dark raisins

1/3 cup (55 g) golden raisins

1/3 cup (55 g) dried currants

1/3 cup (60 g) diced candied orange peel

1/4 cup (50 g) Demerara sugar

2 tablespoons unsalted butter, melted and cooled

Juice of 1/2 lemon

1/2 teaspoon mixed spice

Pinch of salt

Recipe continues on the following page

Continued from the previous page

On a lightly floured work surface, roll out the pastry into a large round about ⅛ inch (3 mm) thick. Using a 3¼-inch (8-cm) fluted cookie cutter, cut out 12 rounds. Transfer the rounds to the prepared pan wells, pressing them gently onto the bottom and up the sides. Spoon about 2 teaspoons mincemeat into each pastry shell, spreading it evenly. Gather up the pastry scraps, press together, and reroll the same way. Using a plain round cookie cutter in the diameter of the top of the pan well (about 2½ inches/6 cm for a fairy cake pan or muffin pan), cut out a lid for each pie. Top each pie with a lid, pressing gently at the edges to seal to the bottom pastry. Using the tip of a sharp knife, cut a small hole in the center of each lid. If you prefer, you can use a star-shape cutter in the same size for the lids, omitting the holes.

Bake the pies until the pastry is golden brown and the filling is cooked through, 12–15 minutes. Let cool in the pan on a wire rack for at least 10 minutes, then serve warm or at room temperature. Use the tip of a small knife to ease each pie out of the pan.

 1960s SPIN *Mincemeat isn't just for small tarts. Famed 1960s television chef and writer Fanny Cradock suggested making giant mince pies, calling the small version "nasty little things which men hate." For a period-specific twist, you could also try a mincemeat Swiss (jelly) roll, mincemeat meringue pie, or even a mincemeat omelet (flambéed, of course).*

FOR THE PASTRY

2 cups (250 g) flour, plus more for the work surface

1 tablespoon granulated sugar

½ cup plus 2 teaspoons (125 g) cold butter, cut into small cubes, plus more for the pan

1 egg, lightly beaten

3–5 tablespoons (45–60 ml) ice-cold water

VIOLET
You're gonna have to lay off the mince pies, Fred Buckle, or never mind splitting your trousers. You're not gonna fit in this Santa suit at all!

FRED
Well, the kiddies leave them out for me. They'd be disappointed if they didn't disappear.

VIOLET
Yes, but you're not the real Father Christmas remember. You're just one of his helpers.

SEASON 5: CHRISTMAS

CHRISTMAS PUDDING

No British Christmas would be complete without a flaming pudding, and no Call the Midwife *Christmas special would be complete without one lurking in the background (or, as in the Christmas special for season 5, splattered all over the walls and ceiling). This recipe is adapted from the government-sponsored Empire Christmas Pudding, which was launched to great fanfare in the 1920s. The recipe, by Henri Cédard, the head royal chef at the time, was designed to showcase ingredients from across the British Empire, then in its heyday. Cinnamon came from India, raisins from South Africa, sugar from Guyana, and rum from Jamaica. After the war, and the terrible upheavals across the former empire as it disintegrated, many people fled war or simply came to Britain seeking a better life. A number of them settled in the East End, an aspect brilliantly explored as we watch the population of Poplar change across the seasons.*

SERVES 8–10

Butter a 5-cup (1.2-l) plain pudding mold. Cut a round of parchment paper and a round of aluminum foil 3–4 inches (7.5–10 cm) larger than the top of the mold. Butter one side of the parchment.

In a large bowl, combine the currants, golden and dark raisins, bread crumbs, suet, candied peel, flour, sugar, apple, eggs, beer, rum, cinnamon, and mixed spice, and stir until all the ingredients are evenly distributed. Transfer the mixture to the prepared pudding mold. Place the parchment round, buttered side down, on the mold and top with the foil round. Make a narrow pleat across the center of the layered rounds (this will allow the "lid" to expand as the pudding rises during steaming), press the overhang down the sides of the mold, and tie the rounds tightly in place around the rim of the mold with kitchen string. To make a handle to ease lowering and lifting the mold, thread the end of a long length of string under the string on one side of the mold, then thread the other end under the string on the opposite side. Bring the ends together and tie securely, leaving enough slack for the pudding to rise.

Select a saucepan large enough to accommodate the mold with room for circulating steam. Place a trivet or an inverted heatproof saucer on the bottom of the pan and fill the pan with water to reach about 1 inch (2.5 cm) below the rim of the mold once it is added. Bring the water to a boil over high heat and carefully lower the mold into the pan. Let the water return to a full boil, then cover the pan and lower the heat so the water is still bubbling but not so vigorously that it splashes over the top of the pudding.

Steam for 4 hours, topping up the water with boiling water as necessary to maintain the original level. Never let the pan boil dry, as although it is unlikely the mold will explode, it will crack, and your kitchen will fill with smoke. Additionally, if the water gets too low, the pudding won't cook properly.

Butter, for the mold and parchment

⅔ cup (115 g) dried currants

⅔ cup (115 g) golden raisins

⅔ cup (115 g) dark raisins

3 cups (115 g) fresh bread crumbs

¼ lb (115g) shredded suet

⅓ cup (55 g) diced candied orange peel

½ cup (60 g) flour

½ cup (100 g) Demerara sugar

1 eating apple, peeled, cored, and grated on the large holes of a box grater

2 eggs, lightly beaten

½ cup (120 ml) dark beer or stout

2 tablespoons rum or brandy

2 teaspoons ground cinnamon

1 teaspoon mixed spice

TO SERVE

Holly sprig, for decoration

3–4 tablespoons brandy

After 4 hours, turn off the heat, carefully lift the pudding mold from the water, snip the string, and remove the foil and parchment. Invert a serving plate on top of the mold, invert the plate and mold together, and lift off the mold. (You can cook the pudding several days in advance of serving, unmold it as directed, let it cool completely, then cover tightly and refrigerate. When ready to serve. just pop the pudding back into the mold, cover it with fresh layers of buttered parchment and foil, tie the layers in place, and steam for 1 hour to heat through. Or you can set the unmolded pudding on a plate and reheat it in a microwave, which should take about 10 minutes.)

To serve, lay the holly sprig on top of the hot pudding. Just before serving, heat the brandy in a ladle or small saucepan until hot, pour it over the pudding, and immediately—and carefully—ignite it with a long match. Then quickly bear the flaming pudding to the table to glorious acclaim.

RECIPE NOTE This pudding is delicious with custard sauce or heavy cream, but brandy butter is also popular. To make it, in a bowl, using a wooden spoon or a handheld mixer, beat together ½ cup (115 g) unsalted butter, at room temperature, and 2 cups (225g) confectioners' sugar until creamy. Mix in ¼ cup (60 ml) brandy until fully incorporated. Cover and refrigerate to harden, then remove from the refrigerator 30 minutes before serving.

SISTER MONICA JOAN
Now's the time to souse the Christmas pudding!

SISTER EVANGELINA
Just don't go sousing yourself into the bargain. You give us enough gip when you're stone cold sober!

SEASON 5: CHRISTMAS

CHOCOLATE-ORANGE YULE LOG

Both yule logs and their everyday counterpart, Swiss (jelly) rolls, were invented in late nineteenth century France and arrived in the United Kingdom soon after. They quickly became a staple of confectioners and skilled home bakers, as they were cheap to make but satisfyingly flashy to look at. Yule logs appear on the Nonnatus House Christmas table nearly every year, and Swiss rolls are also frequently seen. The flavor combination of chocolate and orange is a contemporary one, though it is more commonly seen in a cake. However, it also reflects the popularity of oranges (and, in the show, tangerines) at Christmas, including in the form of Terry's Chocolate Orange, a UK commercial product that originated in York in the early 1930s and remains a common addition to British Christmas stockings. Be warned: One 1957 writer pointedly remarked that the yule log was "hardly a cake for an inexperienced cook to attempt."

If you prefer a nonalcoholic version, substitute fresh orange juice for the liqueur-water mix.

SERVES 8–10

To make the cake, preheat the oven to 400°F (200°C). Butter the bottom and sides of a 13×9×1-inch (33×23×2.5-cm) Swiss (jelly) roll pan and line the bottom with parchment paper.

Pour water to a depth of about 2 inches (5 cm) into a saucepan and bring to a simmer over medium heat. Adjust the heat to maintain a gentle simmer. Rest a heatproof bowl in the rim of the pan, add the eggs, superfine sugar, and orange zest to the bowl, and whisk together until the sugar dissolves and the mixture is thick and creamy and has nearly doubled in volume. Remove the bowl from the pan and continue to whisk the mixture until it cools to lukewarm.

Sift together the flour and baking powder into the egg mixture. Then, using a rubber spatula, fold the flour mixture into the egg mixture just until combined. Transfer the batter to the prepared pan and, using an offset spatula, spread it to fill the corners of the pan, making the middle a little shallower than the edges.

Bake the cake just until the center springs back when lightly pressed with a fingertip and before the edges turn brown, 5–8 minutes.

While the cake is baking, lay a kitchen towel on a work surface and dust it with confectioners' sugar (to prevent the cake from sticking to the towel). When the cake is ready, remove it from the oven, carefully invert the pan onto the sugared towel, and then lift off the pan and peel off the parchment. Cover the cake with a second kitchen towel and let cool completely.

FOR THE CAKE

Butter, for the pan

4 eggs

½ cup (100 g) superfine sugar

Finely grated zest of 1 orange

⅔ cup (85 g) flour

¼ teaspoon baking powder

Confectioners' sugar, for dusting

2 tablespoons triple sec or other orange-flavor liqueur

2 tablespoons water

FOR THE GANACHE

10½ oz (300 g) dark chocolate, roughly chopped

1 cup (240 ml) heavy cream

Finely grated zest of 2 oranges

While the cake is cooling, make the ganache. Put the chocolate into a heatproof bowl. In a small saucepan, combine the cream and orange zest over medium heat and bring to just below the boiling point. Pour the hot cream over the chocolate, let stand for 4–5 minutes to melt, and then stir vigorously until the ganache is thick and shiny. Do not overwork. Let cool slightly until thick enough to spread.

Make a shallow cut or X in one short end of the cake along the side you plan to roll from (this helps with the initial rolling). In a small bowl, stir together the orange liqueur and water and, using a pastry brush, brush the top of the cake lightly with the mixture. Let stand for a few minutes to soak in partially (adding this bit of moisture makes the cake easier to roll). Now spread about one-half of the ganache in an even layer over the surface of the cake, extending it to the edges. Starting from the short end with the cut, and using the towel to help, roll up the cake. Place the cake seam-side down on a serving plate.

Use the remaining ganache to coat the top, sides, and ends of the roll. Then drag a fork through the ganache along the length of the log to create a bark-like effect and use a cocktail stick to create tree ring–like markings on each end. You can serve the cake right away, but it is best chilled for at least 2 hours before serving and can be made up to a day in advance.

 1960s SPIN *Decorate the yule log with meringue mushrooms or plastic holly. For a classier look, use slivers of candied orange peel and a simple dusting of confectioners' sugar added just before serving.*

TRIXIE
Are you staying for tea, Dr. Turner? Mrs. B has made an absolute pièce de résistance of yule log.

SEASON 2: CHRISTMAS

CHRISTMAS CAKE

The British are renowned for their love of dark, fruity flavors at Christmas. This cake is one of a trio of dishes, along with Christmas pudding and mince pies, that has roots in the Middle Ages. Before the advent of cake in the modern sense, fruity breads were part of the festive tradition, evolving slowly into heavy, fruity cakes. Fruit cake was at the heart of every celebratory event, from weddings and christenings to Christmas, though the words Christmas and cake weren't put together properly until the Victorians gave the holiday a good shake-up. For those who aren't a fan of the dark, treacly versions, this one is much lighter. It is based on a recipe in a book by Alma McKee, a Swedish-born chef who became the first woman to head up a royal kitchen when she went to work for the then Princess Elizabeth at Clarence House. When Elizabeth became queen, Mrs. McKee went to cook for the queen mother instead and published a book of her recipes in 1963. This cake would have been very familiar to Princess Margaret, who makes a brief appearance in season 3, opening the new prenatal and baby clinic.

SERVES 12–16

To make the cake, preheat the oven to 275°F (135°C). Butter the bottom and sides of a 9-inch (23-cm) round cake pan, then line the bottom and sides with parchment paper and butter the parchment.

In a bowl, using a wooden spoon, beat together the butter and superfine sugar until light and creamy. Add the marmalade and treacle, and mix until incorporated. Add the egg yolks one at a time alternately with the flour about ⅔ cup (85 g) at a time, mixing well after each addition. (Adding the egg yolks alternately with the flour helps prevent the batter from curdling.) Add the currants, golden and dark raisins, candied peel, nutmeg, salt, rum, and vanilla and almond extracts, and stir until evenly distributed.

In a large bowl, using an electric mixer, beat the egg whites on medium-high speed until stiff peaks form. Working in two or three batches, gently fold the egg whites into the batter just until no white streaks remain.

Transfer the batter to the prepared pan. Wrap the bottom and sides of the pan with a double layer of brown parcel paper and tie the paper in place with kitchen string. Top with a loose lid of parcel paper or aluminum foil.

Bake the cake until the top is golden and a skewer inserted into the center comes out clean, about 3 hours. Begin checking for doneness after 2½ hours. Let cool in the pan on a wire rack about 1 hour, then turn the cake out onto the rack, peel off the parchment, turn upright, and let cool completely.

FOR THE CAKE

1½ cups (340 g) butter, at room temperature, plus more for the pan and parchment

1⅔ cups (340 g) superfine sugar

1½ tablespoons orange marmalade

1 tablespoon black treacle or blackstrap molasses

7 eggs, separated

4 cups (500 g) flour

2 cups (340 g) dried currants

2 cups (340 g) golden raisins

1 cup (170 g) dark raisins

1 cup (170 g) diced candied orange peel

½ teaspoon ground nutmeg

Pinch of salt

1½ tablespoons rum

¾ teaspoon pure vanilla extract

¼ teaspoon pure almond extract

Recipe continues on the following page

Continued from the previous page

To decorate the cake, place it on a flat serving plate or cake pedestal. In a small saucepan, warm the jam over medium-low heat until fluid, then pass the jam through a fine-mesh sieve placed over a small bowl. Using a pastry brush, brush the warm jam over the top and sides of the cake. Sift a light dusting of confectioners' sugar onto a work surface. Set the marzipan on the prepared surface and knead until soft, pliable, and smooth, then flatten it into a thick disk. Lightly dust the disk and a rolling pin with more sugar, and roll out the disk into a round large enough to cover the top and sides of the cake, lifting and rotating it occasionally to make sure it is not sticking to the surface. It should be about ¼ inch (6 mm) thick. Gently roll the marzipan around the rolling pin, then carefully unroll it over the cake, draping it evenly over the top and down the sides. First smooth the top, pressing the marzipan lightly against the cake to force out any air bubbles, and then smooth the sides, gently pulling downward to avoid any ripples or seams. Using a small knife, trim off any excess marzipan from the bottom of the cake. Loosely cover the cake with parchment paper so air can circulate and let stand at room temperature for 2–3 days to allow the marzipan to set and dry.

You can top the marzipan with either royal icing or fondant. If choosing the icing, use an icing spatula to cover the top and sides of the cake, making the icing as smooth or as textured—with peaks and swirls—as you like. If using fondant, handle it the same way you handled the marzipan, first kneading it and rolling it out on a sugar-dusted surface and then smoothing it over the top and sides of the cake. If using icing, you can spoon the remainder into one or more piping bags fitted with decorative tips and fancifully decorate the cake. Any excess fondant can be shaped into ribbons, small balls, flowers, leaves, or other decorations and arranged on the cake. If you like, color the icing or fondant used for decorating with food coloring before piping or shaping. Or you can opt for the more muted Nonnatus House route of plastic figurines and a jolly ribbon tied with a flourish around the sides. Whatever you choose to do, remember that Christmas is no time for tasteful restraint.

RECIPE NOTE Mrs. McKee made her Christmas cakes on November 16, the same day she made her Christmas puddings. Everything would then be packed up and sent to Sandringham for the royal Christmas. The Christmas cake will keep for several weeks wrapped in parchment paper or enclosed in an airtight container and stored at room temperature, which means the cake can be made in advance and then covered with marzipan and icing or fondant at your leisure before serving.

TO DECORATE

½ cup (160 g) apricot jam

Confectioners' sugar, for dusting

2 lb (1 kg) marzipan

2 lb (1 kg) ready-made royal icing or fondant (sugar paste)

Food coloring (optional)

SISTER MONICA JOAN
This contains more fruit than any commercial confectioner's item, and furthermore it is steeped in such a richness of alcohol that it will not fester should you transfer it through the hemisphere.

PATSY
They can't give out Christmas cake in an African vaccination queue. The marzipan would take a tremendous amount of explaining.

SEASON 6: CHRISTMAS

MARSHMALLOW SNOWMAN

The season 8 Christmas special is memorable for the introduction of May, the abandoned Hong Kong orphan who, by the end of the episode, the Turners have decided to take in and foster. We also meet both Sister Mildred and Miss Higgins for the first time. Amid a highly eventful episode that includes an unexpected street-side birth, the reuniting of long-lost siblings, and the election of a new Mother Superior, the customary well-laden Christmas table appears. Unusually, the Christmas spread features this novelty cake, glimpsed first whole and then very enthusiastically demolished a little later on. At the time, several writers published recipes for similar cakes aimed squarely at children. The basic sponge here is incredibly easy. It's known as the all-in-one method of sponge-cake making, and it was the first recipe many children learned, especially after the introduction of the Kenwood Chef in 1950. One of these versatile food mixers is visible at the back of the Turners' kitchen.

SERVES 12-16

To make the sponge, have all the ingredients at room temperature before you start. It is worth making the sponge the day before you assemble the snowman so it has time to cool fully.

Preheat the oven to 350°F (180°C). Butter the bottom and sides of a 6×6-inch (15×15-cm) round springform pan (panettone pan) and a 1¼-cup (300-ml) pudding mold.

Sift together the flour, sugar, and baking powder into the bowl of a stand mixer fitted with the paddle attachment (or you can use a large bowl and a handheld mixer). Add the softened butter, eggs, lemon zest, and lemon extract, and beat on medium speed about 10 minutes. Stop the mixer, scrape down the sides of the bowl with a rubber spatula, and then continue to beat on medium speed for 5 minutes longer. The mixture should be pale, fluffy, and homogenous.

Divide the batter between the prepared pan and mold, starting with the pudding mold. Fill the mold about two-thirds full, smoothing the top with the spatula. Then put the remaining batter into the springform pan and smooth the top. Transfer the cakes to the oven. Bake the smaller cake until a skewer inserted into the center comes out clean, 55–60 minutes. Leave the larger cake in the oven for 10 minutes longer before checking to see if it is done.

When each cake is ready, let cool on a wire rack for 10–15 minutes. Turn the smaller cake out of the mold onto the rack. For the larger cake, unclasp and lift off the sides of the pan, then slide the cake off the pan bottom onto the rack. The top should have peaked slightly, which will help form the snowman's neck. Leave both cakes to cool completely, ideally overnight. If you have space in the fridge, chilling them will make them easier to shape the next day. The sponge should be fairly dense, making it easy to cut and shape.

FOR THE SPONGE

1½ cups (340 g) butter, plus more for the pans

2¾ cups (340 g) flour

1⅔ cups (340 g) superfine sugar

2 teaspoons baking powder

6 eggs

Finely grated zest of 1 lemon

1 teaspoon pure lemon extract

FOR THE ITALIAN MERINGUE BUTTERCREAM

¼ cup (60 ml) water

1 cup (200 g) vanilla sugar (see Recipe Note)

1 tablespoon liquid glucose (optional)

2 egg whites

Pinch of cream of tartar or squeeze of fresh lemon juice

1 cup (225 g) butter, at room temperature

½ teaspoon pure vanilla extract

Recipe continues on the following page

Continued from the previous page

When you are ready to assemble the snowman, make the Italian meringue buttercream. In a small, heavy saucepan, combine the water, vanilla sugar, and liquid glucose (if using) and attach a candy thermometer to the side of the pan. Place over medium heat and heat, without stirring, until the thermometer registers 235°–240°F (113°–116°C), known as the soft-ball stage. If crystals start to form on the sides of the pan, brush them down with a pastry brush dipped in water. While the sugar syrup is heating, in the stand mixer fitted with the whip attachment, beat the egg whites on medium speed until foamy, then add the cream of tartar, increase the speed to medium-high, and beat until soft peaks form.

Now, with the mixer on medium speed, slowly drizzle the hot sugar syrup into the egg whites, being careful not to splash it onto the side of the bowl, where it will set. When all the syrup has been added, increase the mixer speed to medium-high and continue to beat until the mixture is warm (about 100°F/38°C), 3–5 minutes.

At this stage, begin adding the butter. Make sure it is soft and spreadable before you start and that the meringue is still a little warm. With the mixer on medium speed, add the butter, about 2 tablespoons at a time, mixing well after each addition. Once all the butter has been incorporated, add the vanilla and beat until evenly mixed. The buttercream should be smooth, glossy, and spreadable.

To assemble the snowman, first neatly trim the head (the smaller cake) and then round off the top of the body (the larger cake) to make shoulders. Slide the dowel vertically through the center of the body and then carefully slide the head onto the dowel. Once the head is in position, using an offset spatula, frost the entire cake with a thick layer of buttercream. Next, stick the halved marshmallows, cut side down, all over the cake. Color a lump of soft, pliable marzipan with orange food coloring, form it into a carrot shape, and set it in place for the nose. Place chocolate buttons above the nose for the eyes, adhering them with a dab of buttercream. Color a second lump of soft, pliable marzipan with black food coloring, shape it into a hat, and set it on top of the head, attaching it with a dab of buttercream. (Alternatively, use a licorice pinwheel for a hat or cloak the plain marzipan hat in melted chocolate.) Finally, braid some licorice laces or use strips of fruit leather and drape around the neck for a scarf. If you want to add arms, licorice sticks work well, as would chocolate Matchmakers. Use cocktail sticks to secure them in place.

RECIPE NOTE If you don't have vanilla sugar for the buttercream, you can use superfine sugar and add a little extra vanilla extract at the end, though it will make your snowlike buttercream a little muddy-color. It's worth keeping all your scraped or boiled and dried vanilla beans to make vanilla sugar: Just put them in a jar of sugar, cap the jar tightly, and they will soon flavor it. As the sugar is used, replace it. The beans will keep yielding flavor for a surprisingly long time. You can make lavender sugar in a similar way.

1960s SPIN *Don't throw away the cake trimmings. The welfare state is both new and needed, and we see its impact repeatedly throughout the show, but a governmental safety net is no reason for waste. You can use the trimmings to replace some of the bread crumbs in the crumble topping on page 168, or you can add them to the trifle on page 210.*

TO DECORATE

1 narrow wooden dowel, about 8 inches (20 cm) long

20–25 medium marshmallows, cut in half horizontally

Marzipan and orange and black food coloring, for the carrot nose and hat

Chocolate buttons, for the eyes

Licorice laces or fruit leather strips, for the scarf

Licorice sticks or chocolate Matchmakers and cocktail sticks, for arms (optional)

SISTER WINIFRED
One snowman cake, all present and correct!

LUCILLE
What's all that green stuff 'round the edges?

SISTER WINIFRED
It's lime-flavor jelly chopped up to represent grass.

SEASON 8: CHRISTMAS SPECIAL

CARIBBEAN BLACK CAKE

One of the more unusual Christmas recipes to feature in the show, black cake is a specialty of the former British colonies in the West Indies. It's sometimes called Jamaican black cake and sometimes Guyanese, and it's rare to find published recipes before the 1970s. However, its roots almost certainly lie in the rich fruit cakes so loved by the British—the same tradition that gave us the English Christmas cake and the black bun of the Scottish Hogmanay (New Year's celebration), which is still often yeast-risen (and occasionally comes covered in pastry). In the Caribbean, the cake evolved in a different direction, and the result is more like a pudding than a cake: moist, dense, and very dark. The only consistent ingredients are dried fruits macerated in lots of alcohol, the burnt sugar coloring, and the basic flour-butter-egg-sugar mixture of the underlying cake. The piece Lucille and Cyril offer to Sister Monica Joan as she faces a miserable Christmas in St. Cuthbert's probably came from one of the ladies of their church. Each baker would have had her own special twist, and it remains a cake of almost infinite variety.

SERVES 10-12

Start with the macerated fruit. Ideally, you should mix all the fruits and the alcohol together, pack the mixture into a tightly capped jar or other airtight container, and leave the container in a cool cupboard for a year or more. If you don't have a year, combine the currants, raisins, prunes, cherries, and wine in a saucepan and bring to a boil over medium-high heat. Reduce the heat to a simmer, and simmer the mixture for 20 minutes. Remove from the heat, stir in the rum, let cool, cover, and leave at room temperature overnight.

When you are ready to make the cake, put the whole lot into a blender and blend until you have a smooth paste. Set aside.

To make the burnt sugar, in a large, heavy saucepan, heat the sugar over medium heat until it starts to caramelize. Do not stir the sugar until at least two-thirds of it has started to caramelize, and then as you stir with a wooden spoon, be careful not to splatter the pan sides. Keep the pan over medium heat until the sugar is turning a dark brown, starting to smoke, and frothing up the pan sides. In one smooth movement, pour in the boiling water—it will froth up vigorously, so be careful—and stir to combine. Continue to boil gently for 5 minutes, then remove from the heat and set aside to cool and thicken.

FOR THE FRUIT

1¾ cups (300 g) dried currants

¾ cup plus 2 tablespoons (150 g) raisins

¾ cup plus 2 tablespoons (150 g) pitted prunes

⅔ cup (100 g) dried cherries

1¼ cups (300 ml) full-bodied red wine

⅔ cup (160 ml) rum

FOR THE BURNT SUGAR

1 cup plus 2 tablespoons (240 g) firmly packed light brown sugar

1 cup (240 ml) boiling water or full-bodied red wine

To make the cake, preheat the oven to 275°F (135°C). Butter the bottom and sides of a 9-inch (23-cm) round cake pan and line the bottom with parchment paper.

In a large bowl, using an electric mixer, beat together the butter and sugar on medium speed until the mixture is light brown and fluffy. On low speed, add the flour in four batches alternately with the eggs in three batches, beginning and ending with the flour and mixing well after each addition. Add the mixed spice and orange zest, and beat until well mixed. Add the fruit paste and peanuts and finally the burnt sugar syrup, and mix just until evenly distributed. Transfer the batter to the prepared pan.

Bake the cake until the top is set when pressed with a fingertip but the interior is still very moist, about 2½ hours. A skewer inserted into the center should come out with a few moist crumbs attached. Let cool in the pan on a wire rack for 10 minutes. Then, using a pastry brush, brush the top with the rum. You may need to do this in two applications, allowing time for the rum to soak into the cake before adding the remainder. Let the cake cool completely in the pan, then turn it out onto the rack and peel off the parchment.

Wrap the cake in aluminum foil or parchment paper and store at room temperature for at least 1 week or up to 2 weeks before eating. If you feel decadent, brush the top with 1 tablespoon rum for each of the first 3 days to give it an even boozier punch.

At Christmas, black cake is always served undecorated.

RECIPE NOTE This recipe can be varied according to taste. For the fruit, you can use port or stout in place of the wine or all rum. You can also use different dried fruits (though it is best to avoid anything with small seeds, such as figs), and you can omit the nuts.

FOR THE CAKE

1½ cups (340 g) butter, at room temperature, plus more for the pan

1 cup plus 1 tablespoon (220 g) firmly packed light brown sugar

1¾ cups (225 g) flour

6 eggs, lightly beaten

2 teaspoons mixed spice

Finely grated zest of 1 orange

¾ cup (115 g) unsalted roasted peanuts, coarsely chopped

TO FINISH

3 tablespoons rum, plus 3 tablespoons for daily feeding (optional)

CYRIL
How about Lucille and I come and see you and bring some tangerines and a bit of black bun?
SEASON 10:
CHRISTMAS
SPECIAL

NUT ROAST WITH CHESTNUT STUFFING

Vegetarianism has a very long history, though the term itself is less than two hundred years old. It wasn't until the late nineteenth century that the modern movement, largely secular and with an emphasis on animal welfare, was founded. At that time, it had strong links to the suffrage movement as well and was associated particularly with women. By the 1960s, it was still not mainstream, though it was growing, and the period saw the publication of a number of vegetarian cookery books and an upsurge in interest. Vegetarians got a pretty raw deal. The British attitude toward vegetables was to boil them to death and serve them, if you were lucky, with butter or white sauce. Putting them at the center of a spread was unthinkable. Most meat was still very expensive and therefore privileged. Vegetarian cuisine involved a lot of vegetable gravy, tomato sauce, pasta, and cheese. Occasionally, more elaborate dishes crept in, including the ubiquitous Christmas nut roast (often called nut savory), which was a mixture of Edwardian-style stuffing with lessons from the war and its meat shortages. These nut roasts were usually bland and stodgy, an afterthought for the single vegetarian needing to be catered to at Christmas. This one has been somewhat modernized to improve it.

SERVES 6–8 AS A MAIN COURSE

To make the stuffing, in a frying pan, heat the oil over medium heat. Add the onion and cook, stirring occasionally, until softened and translucent, 3–5 minutes. Add the bread crumbs, chestnuts, bouillon powder, sage, thyme, and soy sauce, and stir to mix well. Remove from the heat and set aside.

To make the nut roast, in a frying pan, heat the oil over medium heat. Add the onion and cook, stirring occasionally, until browned, 8–10 minutes. While the onion is cooking, measure 1/2 cup (120 g) of the tomatoes for the roast and set the remainder aside for the sauce. When the onion is browned, add the tomatoes, flour, bouillon powder, water, and soy sauce, and cook over medium heat, stirring often, until the mixture comes together as a thick sauce, about 10 minutes. Set aside to cool.

In a dry frying pan, heat the walnuts and cashews over medium heat, stirring occasionally, until toasted and fragrant, 4–5 minutes. Pour onto a cutting board and let cool.

Chop the cooled nuts and transfer to a bowl. Add the bread crumbs, herb blend, and cheese, and stir to mix well. Add the cooled tomato mixture and stir to combine. Season with salt and pepper.

FOR THE CHESTNUT STUFFING

2 tablespoons vegetable oil

1 yellow onion, finely chopped

1 1/2 cups (60 g) fresh whole-wheat bread crumbs

1 cup (115 g) jarred or vacuum-packed roasted and peeled cooked chestnuts, finely chopped

1 tablespoon vegetable bouillon powder

1 teaspoon dried sage

1 teaspoon dried thyme

2 tablespoons soy sauce

Add just enough of the beaten eggs to the stuffing, stirring as you go, until it becomes moist enough to hold together. Stir the remaining egg into the chestnut stuffing.

Preheat the oven to 350°F (180°C). Butter the bottom and sides of an 8½×4½-inch (21.5×11.5-cm) loaf pan. Line the bottom and sides of the pan with parchment paper, leaving enough overhang on the pan sides to cover the top of the roast.

If you want to add an oat crust, coat the parchment (not the overhang) with the butter, then pat the rolled oats evenly over the buttered surface, making sure the bottom and sides are evenly and completely covered. Otherwise, skip this step.

Spoon two-thirds of the nut mixture into the prepared loaf pan and press it onto the bottom and sides in a layer ½ inch (12 mm) thick. Spoon the chestnut stuffing into the nut-mixture shell and press down firmly. Spoon the remaining nut mixture over the stuffing and smooth the surface. Fold the excess parchment over the top of the roast, then cover the pan with aluminum foil.

Bake the nut roast, rotating the pan back to front after 30 minutes to ensure even baking, for 1 hour.

While the nut roast is baking, make the tomato sauce. In a small saucepan, combine the tomatoes, apple, and onion, and bring to a simmer over medium heat. Simmer, stirring occasionally, until the apple and onion soften and the tomatoes begin to break down, about 10 minutes. Remove from the heat, let cool slightly, transfer to a blender, and blend until smooth, then return to the pan. Alternatively, blend until smooth in the pan using an immersion blender. Add the tomato paste, sugar, ginger, cloves, and vinegar to the tomato mixture and season with salt and pepper. Return the pan to medium heat and simmer the sauce, stirring occasionally, until thickened, about 10 minutes. Taste and adjust with more sugar or vinegar and with salt and pepper if needed.

Remove the nut roast from the oven and let rest, still covered, for 10 minutes. Remove the foil and unfold the parchment. Invert a serving dish or platter on top of the loaf pan and then carefully invert the pan and plate together. Lift off the pan and peel off the parchment.

Serve with the tomato sauce in a jug on the side. Remember, this is a Christmas dish, so a certain flourish (and a festive plate) is encouraged.

FOR THE NUT ROAST

2 tablespoons vegetable oil

1 yellow onion, finely chopped

1 can (14 oz/400 g) diced tomatoes

2 tablespoons flour

1 tablespoon vegetable bouillon powder

⅔ cup (160 ml) water

1 tablespoon soy sauce

1 cup (115 g) raw walnuts

1 cup (115 g) raw cashews

2¾ cups (110 g) fresh whole-wheat bread crumbs

1 tablespoon dried Italian herb blend

1 cup (115 g) grated sharp Cheddar cheese

Salt and pepper

2 eggs, lightly beaten

Butter, for the pan

FOR THE OAT CRUST (OPTIONAL)

2 tablespoons butter, at room temperature

⅔ cup (65 g) rolled oats

FOR THE TOMATO SAUCE

Diced tomatoes, remaining from the nut roast

1 small tart apple, peeled, cored, and finely chopped

1 small yellow onion, finely chopped

2 tablespoons tomato paste (UK purée)

3 tablespoons firmly packed brown sugar

½ teaspoon ground ginger

¼ teaspoon ground cloves

⅔ cup (160 ml) malt vinegar

Salt and pepper

TRIFLE

Trifle is one of the more frequently seen sweet dishes at Nonnatus House. It's very much a celebratory dish, most often appearing at Christmas or as part of a party spread. It's peculiarly British, having eighteenth century origins but becoming wildly popular from the late Victorian era onward. By the 1950s, there were hundreds of variations, with every household swearing its version was the best. When good, it's a real crowd-pleaser. When bad—many 1960s versions definitely fall into this category—it's a terrible cacophony of soggy cake and bland cream. This recipe is based on a 1920s trifle from the evocatively titled The Gentle Art of Cookery. *It's the kind of trifle Miss Higgins would have grown up with. In the season 10 Christmas special, it's the dish she sits down to at her ideal Christmas dinner, joyously celebrated with Phyllis Crane.*

SERVES 6

Drain the peaches into a fine-mesh sieve over a small, heavy saucepan. Set the peaches aside. Add the granulated sugar to the syrup, bring to a boil over medium-high heat, and boil for a few minutes until the syrup thickens slightly. Remove from the heat, stir in the vanilla, if using, and let cool to room temperature.

Cut the fairy cakes into even slices about ½ inch (1 cm) thick. Arrange the slices on the bottom of a 2½- to 3-quart (2- to 3-liter) clear glass bowl. Top with the macaroons and ratafias in a single layer. Drizzle the sherry evenly over the biscuits, adding just enough to moisten them. You do not want them to break down. Pour the cooled peach syrup evenly over the top, and top with the drained peaches, arranging them attractively. If you like, reserve a few slices for decorating the top.

In a bowl, using a whisk or an electric mixer on medium-high speed, beat together the cream and confectioners' sugar until stiff peaks form. Spoon the cream into a piping bag fitted with a plain or star tip and pipe the cream over the peaches, or simply spoon the cream gently and attractively over the peaches. Decorate with gay abandon as you like, using the suggestions given here or your own favorites. And if you are feeling particularly festive and daring, serve with a round of Harvey Wallbangers, a cocktail Miss Higgins recalls first drinking in the mid-1920s and champions as the ideal accompaniment to the trifle. Chill for several hours before serving.

1 can (1 lb/450 g) sliced peaches in heavy syrup

1 tablespoon granulated sugar

3–4 drops pure vanilla extract (optional)

6 fairy cakes, or ½ small (6-inch/15-cm) sponge cake

2 oz (60 g) macaroons

2 oz (60 g) ratafia or amaretti biscuits

4–5 tablespoons sherry

1 cup plus 2 tablespoons (300 ml) heavy cream

1½ teaspoons confectioners' sugar

TO DECORATE

Glacé cherries, crystallized flowers, sliced almonds, silver balls, and/or hundreds and thousands

TO SERVE (OPTIONAL)

Harvey Wallbangers

1960s SPIN *Trifles are made in all sorts of designs, and much of the wow factor comes from the decoration. Cookery writer and broadcaster Marguerite Patten, a household name in Britain in the 1960s, published a "crisscross" trifle recipe made of the usual sherry-soaked sponge, canned pears, optional sherry jelly, and a topping of custard, onto which was piped a completed noughts-and-crosses (tic-tac-toe) game.*

A CALL THE MIDWIFE CANAPÉ PARTY

It's easy to prepare low-key dishes for a Nonnatus House dinner or high tea. But if you really want to celebrate the series in style, you need more than just cold meats and a layer cake. For a true taste of the 1950s and 1960s, take a leaf out of Shelagh Turner's book and throw yourself into hosting a canapé party.

Firstly, get the décor right. Canapé parties can be seated, but they can also be standing, with the food displayed buffet-style on whatever tables you have. When the Turners hold their parties, the food is on low coffee tables. But we also see several parties—Lucille and Cyril's wedding among them—in rented halls with food on trestles, and even at Nonnatus House, where the food is on the everyday dining table. Cloths are optional but a good idea: The brighter the better, and be sure to include napkins.

Don't forget the drinks. You can go for cocktails, Babycham (sparkling pear cider), sherry, or fizzy beverages. The average Brit went through only six bottles of wine a year in 1960, but this is probably the ideal occasion to open one. Pick a German Riesling to be truly in the spirit (see 1960s Spin, page 104).

The ideal party food does not require knives and forks, but you should lay in a supply of cocktail sticks and put out small bowls for discarding seeds and peels as well as used sticks. And remember, just putting things on plates is so 1940s. If you can dream it, you can do it.

THINGS ON STICKS

Cheddar cheese and pineapple (it simply isn't a 1960s party without them)

Sausage meatballs, preferably glazed with cocktail sauce (tomato ketchup boosted with some Worcestershire sauce and Tabasco)

Gouda or Edam cheese with fruit (grapes or apple chunks)

Ham wrapped around (tinned) asparagus

Bacon wrapped around prunes (devils on horseback), oysters (angels on horseback), shrimp, orange sections, or gherkins and broiled, with chutney or mustard on the side

You can lay the loaded sticks on platters, but it is better to wrap half of an orange or grapefruit in aluminum foil, set it on a plate, and stick the sticks into it.

Dippers on Sticks: Cut the top off a pineapple and hollow out the center. Fill the pineapple with a dip made from mayonnaise and whipped cream seasoned with some mustard and minced fresh herbs. Then stick things to dip on cocktail sticks—olives, cheese, fruit, shrimp, ham, and so on—and stick the sticks into the pineapple.

THINGS ON BISCUITS

For the biscuits, you can use flaky pastry, savory biscuit mix, scones, or, even better, cheese pastry. Roll out, cut into shapes, bake, and cool. Or you can use toasted bread cut into shapes. Spread the biscuits with one of the following toppings:

Cream cheese mixed with finely chopped ham or pineapple

Shrimp with capers or tomatoes

Pâté or fish mousse

Devil mixture (tomato, Worcestershire sauce, cayenne pepper, and a little olive oil), then broil or fry the biscuits

Blue cheese and thin celery slices

Flavored butters

STUFFED EGGS

A classic and always popular, stuffed eggs are easy to make. Simply lightly hard-boil eggs (5 minutes should do it), then cool, peel, halve lengthwise, and scoop out the yolks into a bowl. Mix the yolks with flavorings, such as minced anchovy fillets, curry powder, and a little cream; mayonnaise, English mustard, smoked paprika, and minced fresh chives; or smoked fish, grated cheese, and a tiny bit of mustard. Form the mixture into yolk-size balls and put the balls into the egg white halves. You can pipe mayonnaise or curl an anchovy fillet around the filling for extra flair.

VOL-AU-VENTS

Fill small baked puff pastry cases with one of the following fillings:

Cream cheese and olives

Cream cheese and walnuts

Coronation chicken (a sauce of minced onion, curry powder, tomato paste [UK purée], red wine, water, and lemon juice, much reduced, then strained, cooled, and mixed with cooked chicken chunks, finely chopped dried apricots, mayonnaise, and a little whipped cream)

Ham or fish mousse

OTHER SAVORY IDEAS

You can go to town with sandwiches (see page 134). Make them in interesting shapes—playing cards are particularly snazzy—so they stand out on the table.

A cheese board and a bowl of fruit are welcome choices, as are small tartlets or a large flan cut into easily handled slices. Some authors even suggest that pizza is a good—if daring—option, easily made with sieved canned tomatoes, anchovy fillets, and Parmesan atop a simple bread-dough base.

SWEETS

For sweets, opt for items easily eaten without recourse to cutlery, such as small cakes or tartlets, iced biscuits, or any of the small sweets included in this book.

VALERIE
We thought we ought to make an effort. Mrs Turner's been planning her canapes for weeks.

LUCILLE
She's doing hard boiled eggs stuffed with kipper mousse and cheese and pineapple on sticks.

SISTER JULIENNE
Ah, that all sounds very modern!

TRIXIE
The Brook Advisory Centre's very modern. And if a range of canapes helps to rally support for a branch in our borough, I happen to think that's all to the good.

SEASON 8: EPISODE 7

BIBLIOGRAPHY

Cookery sources consulted in the writing of the recipe chapters

Dorothy Allhusen, *A Book Of Scents And Dishes* (1927)

Isobel Barnett, *Lady Barnett's Cookbook* (1969)

Isabella Beeton/Ward, Lock & Co., *Mrs Beeton's Book of Household Management* (1961)

Be-Ro, *Be-Ro Home Recipes* (20th edition; 1957)

Arabella Boxer, *First Slice Your Cookbook* (1964)

British Medical Association, *Doctors' Orders* (c.1955)

Catherine Brown, *Broths to Bannocks: Cooking in Scotland 1690 to the Present Day* (1990)

Marjorie Bruce-Milne, ed., *Home Catering and Cookery* (1956)

David Canter, Kay Canter, and Daphne Swann, *The Cranks Recipe Book* (1985)

Elizabeth Craig, *Banana Dishes* (1962)

F. Marian McNeill, *The Scots Kitchen* (1929)

Patty Fisher, *500 Recipes for Vegetarian Cookery* (1969)

Nina Froud, *The World Book of Egg and Cheese Dishes* (1967)

Good Housekeeping Institute, *A Good Housekeeping Cookery Compendium* (1955)

Peter Gray, *The Mistress Cook* (1956)

William Heptinstall, *Hors d'Oeuvre and Cold Table* (1959)

Margaret Hudson, *The Mixer Book* (1972)

Peggy Hutchinson, *Home-Made Cake, Pastry and Biscuit Secrets* (c. 1950)

Susan King, various cookery columns and features in *Woman's Realm* magazine (1960–68)

Mrs. E. W. Kirk, *Tried Favourites Cookery Book* (1929)

Georgina Landemare, *Recipes from No. 10* (1958)

Lily MacLeod, *Cooking for the Wayward Diabetic* (1960)

Gertrude Mann, *A Book of Cakes* (1957)

Alma McKee, *To Set Before a Queen* (1963)

George Newnes, Ltd., *Woman's Own Cook Book* (1964)

Marguerite Patten, *Cookery in Colour* (1960)

Edouard de Pomiane, *Cooking with Pomiane*, trans. Bruno Cassirer (1962)

Princess Gardens School (Belfast, Northern Ireland), *Chefs Galore* (1965)

George and Cecilia Scurfield, *Home Baked* (1956)

Zena Skinner, *Third Book of Recipes* (1966)

Delia Smith, *How to Cheat at Cooking* (1971)

Nancy Spain, *The Nancy Spain Colour Cookery Book* (1963)

Thomas R. Tear, *The Baker's Repository of Recipes* (1947)

Sources consulted in the writing of the essays and headnotes

Stephen McGann, *Call the Midwife: A Labour of Love* (2021)

Heidi Thomas, *The Life and Times of Call the Midwife* (2012)

Jennifer Worth, *The Midwife Trilogy* (2010)

ACKNOWLEDGMENTS

This book was written and tested at breakneck speed with a lot of enthusiastic help. It was an utter joy to write. Thanks are due to all the following people.

For research and recipe testing: Miranda Quantrill, Mary-Ann Boermans, and Keira Andrews. For help with finding books on cake: Janet Clarke and Kira Dietz of the Food Timeline at Virginia Tech.

For supplying recipes and pamphlets while also commenting on the 1960s and all its culinary delights (not just cake): Kate Chapman, Chris Chapman, Mike Gray, Marion Howling, Ian Sutton, and Betty Harris. (And for sending me plastic reindeer: Helen Lane.)

For tasting, quite exhaustively, a lot of cake: Rebecca and Charlie Harris-Quigg (sorry to your then-unborn Quigglets, who may well now be addicted to icing) and Georgina Landick.

For coming to a CTM talk with me even though she'd never watched the series and for eating lots of cake: Kathy Hipperson.

For allowing me, politely, to wave my arms about while talking about cake: Rebecca Lane, KJ and Rich Boardman-Hims, and Jess and Richard Gray. And for involved discussions about iced buns and gingerbread and much else besides: Regula Ysewijn.

For much of the above and for enthusiastically giving two small gingerbread midwives (one lacking a head) a home: my agent, Tim Bates. His colleagues at PFD, Annabel Merullo and Daisy Chandley, also deserve thanks (sorry I didn't give you gingerbread as well).

At Weldon Owen, my editor, Amy Marr, plus the team of Jourdan Plautz and Roger Shaw have been very supportive in the face of me driveling on about silver balls. Thanks to copyeditor Sharon Silva. Thanks also to Ken Carlson, Jennifer Peterson, and Carrie Truesdell at Waterbury Publications.

Everyone at Neal Street has been brilliant: Caroline Reynolds, Pippa Harris, and especially the fabulous Heidi Thomas.

Finally, as always, thanks to Matt Howling, and I'm sorry about the Knickerbocker glories on a school night—and obviously, all the endless cake.

INDEX

weldon**owen**

PO Box 3088
San Rafael, CA 94912
www.weldonowen.com

WELDON OWEN INTERNATIONAL
CEO Raoul Goff
Publisher Roger Shaw
Associate Publisher Amy Marr
Editorial Director Katie Killebrew
Assistant Editor Jourdan Plautz
VP of Creative Chrissy Kwasnik
Senior Production Manager Joshua Smith
Sr Production Manager, Subsidiary Rights Lina s Palma-Temena

Photography Waterbury Publications, Des Moines, IA
Food Stylist Jennifer Peterson

A WELDON OWEN PRODUCTION

Printed and bound in China

All rights reserved. No part of this book may be reproduced in
any form without written permission from the publisher.

First printed in 2023
10 9 8 7 6 5 4 3 2 1

Library of Congress Cataloging in Publication data is available

ISBN: 978-1-68188-828-6

Weldon Owen would also like to thank Sharon Silva and Peggy Fallon.